THE DAY AFTER THE FAIR

by
FRANK HARVEY

based on the short story
On the Western Circuit
by THOMAS HARDY

SAMUEL FRENCH

LONDON
NEW YORK TORONTO SYDNEY HOLLYWOOD

THE DAY AFTER THE FAIR

First presented by Frith Banbury with Jimmy Wax by arrangement with Arthur Cantor on 4th October 1972, at the Lyric Theatre, London, with the following cast of characters:

Edith Harnham	Deborah Kerr
Arthur Harnham	Duncan Lamont
Letty Harnham	Avice Landon
Anna	Julia Foster
Charles Bradford	Paul Hastings
Sarah	Jiggy Bhore

Directed by Frith Banbury

Décor by Reece Pemberton

Lighting by Joe Davis

The action passes in the front room of The Brewer's House, in a west country cathedral city

ACT I
  Scene 1 A May evening
  Scene 2 Morning, ten days later
  Scene 3 Sunday evening, six weeks later

ACT II
  Scene 1 Saturday afternoon, about two
               weeks later
  Scene 2 Three days later
  Scene 3 The morning of the wedding

Time – the late 19th century

ACT I

Scene 1

The front room of "The Brewer's House", in a west country cathedral city.

It is still a handsome room, although now its Georgian proportions have to a large extent become overlaid by Victorian drapes and an excess of furniture and bric-a-brac. Above the study door, heavily curtained sash-windows look out at the market square; in the opposite wall, an archway reveals the entrance hall, part of the staircase and a further door leading to the dining-room. Prominently placed is a portrait of Arthur Harnham's great-grandfather, founder of the brewery and the family fortune. Many of the other paintings in the room are of fine Clydesdale horses, and several silver cups and trophies which record their successes on the showground are displayed in a convenient Georgian niche. Almost the only feminine note in the room is struck by a small but elegant Sheraton desk which stands between the windows and the study door

When the Curtain rises, it is a little before sunset. In the market square outside, a fair is in full swing, and gay, brazen music from a steam-organ is filling the room with sound. Miss Harnham (Letty) stands at a table behind the sofa with a coffee-cup and saucer in her hands. Although she is nearing sixty, she is still a forceful, attractive woman. She moves towards the window, and for a moment or two her attention is held by some distant activity in the square. She moves her head from one position to another to obtain the best view. Suddenly, as someone apparently passes quickly along the pavement outside she moves close to the window and peers out. Arthur Harnham lets himself in through the front door and appears in the hallway. In his middle fifties, red-faced and solidly built, he is the third of his line to hold the chairmanship of Harnham's Brewery. Still carrying his hat and a sheaf of papers, he comes excitedly to Letty. To be heard above the racket from the steam-organ he is obliged to raise his voice

Arthur Well, we've put in a bid, Letty. We've made them an offer.

Letty (*pleased and excited*) You haven't!

Arthur Yes—and the board's behind it one hundred per cent. There wasn't a voice against me.

Letty Oh, Arthur! How splendid!

Arthur Mind you, it means a lot of—here, half a minute, Letty, I can't compete with this.

He goes to shut the window, but Letty intercepts him

Letty I'll do it.

Arthur returns to the hallway and puts his hat on the hall table. Meanwhile, Letty crosses to the window and closes the lower sashes, which reduces the sound of the steam-organ to a tolerable level

Arthur These wretched fair people, they seem determined to make more din every time they come here. Anyhow, I'm raising this matter at the next meeting of the City Council. Something's got to be done, it's becoming quite intolerable.

Letty There!

Arthur That's better. Now—what I was saying is it means a lot of money —an awful lot of money, but it's the right decision, I'm certain.

Letty Oh, I'm sure it is, Arthur. You've been right so many times. The board knows that.

Arthur What would you give to see Tremlett's face? He'll get it in the morning.

Letty I'd give more to have seen Father's. Oh, if only Father could have known this, Arthur.

Arthur Yes. If someone had told him that in less than ten years Harnham's Brewery would be making a bid for Tremlett's he'd have thought they were barmy.

Letty It would have seemed utterly impossible to Father. But what will happen now, Arthur? Will there be a battle?

Arthur Tremlett's getting old. He'll be ready to settle, but there's a son, you know, and I dare say the boy'll try to fight us as long as he can. But I don't care. That's my world and I know where I am in it. Ah, there you are, Edith. I was just telling Letty . . .

Edith Harnham, dressed to go out, comes down the stairs and enters. Younger than Arthur, she is a gentle, attractive creature with a certain nervous vitality suggesting concealed tension

Edith I'm sorry, Arthur. I heard you come in, but I'm just slipping over to the fair for a moment.

Arthur (*incredulous*) To the *fair*? What on earth for?

Edith To look for Anna.

Arthur Anna? Oh, you mean the *new* girl. What's she doing over at the fair?

Edith She had permission, but she should have been back long before this. I'm very cross with her.

Letty Arthur's had a most successful meeting, Edith.

Edith Have you, Arthur? Well, I won't stop now. You must tell me about it when I come in. I shan't be many minutes. It's really too bad of Anna.

Edith goes off and the front door is heard to close behind her

Arthur Hasn't this girl any work to do? The other servants aren't allowed to go gallivanting off whenever the fancy takes them. (*He pours himself a sherry*)

Letty The other servants aren't quite . . .

Arthur Well? Aren't quite what?

Letty Quite in Anna's position, I suppose.

Arthur Either the girl's a servant or she's not. And if she's not, then what the devil's she doing here?

Letty Edith wanted her here. She was interested in the child, she said, and was anxious to help her.

Arthur Oh? Help her do what?

Letty Why, better herself, I suppose you'd call it. It's easily understood when you consider both their families lived in that same village for so long. I gather Edith was friendly with the elder girl when Anna was just a toddler.

Arthur That's all very well among village kids, but one doesn't usually continue with that sort of friendship in adult life, Letty.

Letty Edith says the child needs her, but it's quite clear to me that it's the other way round.

Arthur What do you mean?

Letty Surely it's Edith who needs something to occupy *her.*

Arthur After three years of marriage, I'd have thought she'd have found that among our own circle without having to cultivate the peasantry. (*With sudden irritation*) Who said the girl could go off in the first place? Did you?

Letty No. I told her she couldn't go. So of course she went to Edith and in the end, Edith said she could—just for twenty minutes. But that was over an hour ago.

Arthur Do you mean that Edith gave her permission knowing that you'd already refused it?

Letty (*avoiding a direct answer*) Well—the trouble is, having let one go, now they all want to go, you see.

Arthur That was very wrong of Edith, Letty, and I shall make a point of telling her so.

Letty But, Arthur, she's every right as your wife to expect to be mistress in her own house.

Arthur Well, and so she is, isn't she?

Letty How can she be if she's not allowed the slightest responsibility in the running of it?

Arthur Because that's something you've done ever since Mother died. Everything here runs like a clock.

Letty There's no need to butter me up. I'm not obliged to stay here. Edith's an immensely capable person, Arthur. You'd only to see the way she managed in that frightful old vicarage—practically on a shoe-string.

Arthur (*growing exasperated*) But damn it all, Letty, it was agreed right at the outset, wasn't it? Edith was delighted for you to stay and carry on. She agreed, didn't she? You both did.

Letty I only agreed then because I naturally expected there'd be babies coming along and that Edith would have her hands full. But that hasn't happened, has it?

Arthur (*with whom this is a sore point*) No.

Letty And the result is, she simply hasn't enough to *do*, Arthur.

Arthur Well, to me it's always seemed an ideal arrangement.

Letty Because you don't see further than the end of your nose. You never did.

Sarah, one of the housemaids, appears in the hall

Yes, Sarah? What is it?

Sarah Cook says shall she dish up for the master now, ma'am?

Arthur Just five minutes, tell her. (*To Letty, as he goes*) You haven't waited, I hope?

Letty No—you did *say* you'd be late, Arthur.

Arthur goes off up the stairs

Sarah The water's boiling hot again in the cylinder, ma'am. I come out of the master's room and went into madam's to turn the bed down when it started up that horrible shaking noise. So down the back stairs I goes as fast as I could and shoved all the dampers in quick.

Letty Well done!

Sarah Only I mean they keep saying about these boilers blowing up all over the place, don't they, ma'am?

Letty The truth is, Cook's never understood that old range. She pretends she does, but she doesn't.

There is the sound of the front door opening and closing as Edith returns. She pulls off her gloves and unpins her hat, which, together with her bag, cape and gloves, she hands to Sarah as she speaks

Edith There! I wasn't long, was I? Sarah, when Anna comes back, and she'll be in presently, you're to tell her I want to see her at once.

Sarah Yes, ma'am.

Edith Here. And she's to come just as she is.

Sarah Yes, ma'am.

Sarah goes out with Edith's things and off up the stairs

Edith Was Arthur cross with me for going out?

Letty Of course not. So you were able to find Anna then?

Edith I guessed where she'd be, of course. The great attraction is this new steam roundabout, and I must say it's a most gorgeous sight, Letty. The horses are in threes, you know, and they really seem to be actually galloping. As they go whirling round, each horse in turn rises up into the air and then sinks down again in the most graceful manner you could ever imagine. And all the colours are so new and bright—and everything's reflected a hundred times over in great mirrors. It's all done by steam. The whole effect is quite exhilarating. I found it very difficult to stand there and look cross.

Letty And Anna?

Edith Anna was in paradise. I could tell from the look on her face. And the funny thing was, Letty, as I watched her perched up on the back of this great white horse, I suddenly realized that all the excitement and the strange sensations of motion, they were mine just as much as they were Anna's. It was as if I'd been sitting up there beside her. Quite odd.

Letty But what excuse had she? Was she so carried away that she lost all sense of time?

Edith Not entirely. There was a young man involved.

Letty A young man? Really?

Arthur has come briskly down the stairs into the room

Arthur (*entering*) Do you remember, Letty, the first time *we* ever went to the fair?

Letty Oh, dear me! That's nearly fifty years ago.

Arthur Father took us, and I wasn't allowed to let go of his hand. That's how old *I* was. (*He helps himself to more sherry*)

Letty Yes—but everything was so different—no roundabouts or things of that sort. There were waxworks, I remember, and a peep-show and toys and gingerbread . . .

Arthur And the quack-doctors. Wasn't there some fellow who reckoned to cure the cataract? They said he had his own special way of licking round a person's eyeball and his tongue was as rough as a tom-cat's.

Edith Arthur, how horrible!

Arthur It worked for some of them—came clean away like the skin off a glass of hot milk. But what interested Father were the horses, of course. That was the real business of the fair then—horses. I was just saying to Letty how Father would have enjoyed himself if he'd been at the meeting today.

Letty Oh, wouldn't he!

Arthur (*to Edith*) You see, in Father's time, Tremlett's were on top—right on top. And didn't they let us know it? Well, now it's a different story.

Letty How you've worked, Arthur!

Arthur It's never seemed like work to me. After all, brewing's an art, isn't it? Despite all these clever fellers trying to turn it into a science. Mind you, they never will—not until they find out the secret of life itself, because that's what it's all about. There—on the floor of the maltings that *is* life. And never mind what these chemists *say*, they can't tell you *how* it works and they can't tell you *why* it works.

Letty But you must feel a great sense of achievement, Arthur.

Arthur Well—yes. These are early days, I know, but I must say it does look now as if at last we've got Tremletts where we want them.

Edith (*tentatively*) And that *is* good news, isn't it, Arthur?

Arthur What? It certainly is. Damned good news.

Edith Oh well—then—if you're pleased I'm delighted for you.

Arthur It'll make Harnham's the biggest brewery in the county. Isn't that something to be pleased about?

Edith Yes, yes, of course, I'm sure it is. I only wish I didn't find business affairs so—so incomprehensible.

Arthur My dear girl, business is simply another word for common sense. You have to know your job, of course, and part of my job is to buy barley—at the right price. That's all it is.

Sarah appears in the hall

Letty Yes, Sarah?

Sarah The master's soup's on the table, ma'am.

Arthur I'm coming, I'm coming.

Sarah Only Cook's bursting herself to get done and get out, sir.

Arthur goes off towards the dining-room, followed by Sarah

Arthur (*as he goes*) I suppose it's the fair, eh? We all want to go to the fair, do we?

Edith Oh, dear! How difficult it is to say the right thing.

Letty Well, I'm afraid you make it difficult, Edith. Harnham's has always been a family concern, and I'm sure all Arthur wants is that you should feel you're a part of it.

Edith I do try, Letty, I do try.

Letty (*after a disapproving pause*) You were telling me about Anna and a young man . . .

Edith That girl should certainly have come in by now. And one of the first things I mean to discover is just how they got to know each other.

Letty But surely young people of that class, enjoying themselves at the fair, don't wait on formal introductions.

Edith But you don't understand, Letty. This young man is not one of our local hobbledehoys.

Letty Oh?

Edith Oh! No, no, By no means. He's—well—quite . . .

Letty A gentleman?

Edith Oh yes, that, certainly. And young, very young—but nice.

Letty You met him then?

Edith What happened was that Anna's horse finally stopped quite near me, and as she climbed down, I said to her, "How can you be such a wild girl, Anna? You know you were only to have twenty minutes."

Letty And what did she say?

Edith She looked completely blank. I might have been someone from another world. Then this young man came from behind me and said, "Please, don't blame her. It was entirely my fault. She looked so delightful on the horse that I persuaded her to go round again."

Letty Anna wouldn't need much persuading.

Edith "I assure you," he said, "she's been quite safe." Well, what could I say?

Letty What did you say?

Edith I said, "In that case, I'll leave her in your hands, but I expect her back directly." What the young man must have thought of me, I daren't think.

Letty How do you mean?

Edith Well, I was cross. I spoke so sharply.

Letty But of course you did. And quite rightly so.

Edith I must have made a thoroughly disagreeable impression on him.

Letty I really don't think that need worry *you*, Edith.

Edith No—anyway—I'm sure she *will* be back directly.

Letty Well—I hope you'll be very firm . . .

Anna I am back, ma'am.

Both women turn quickly to find Anna, dressed in her best clothes and wearing hat and gloves, standing in the doorway. She is a radiant eighteen

Edith Ah! Come here, Anna. Why, you look quite flushed.

Anna I expect it was the horses, ma'am. You never felt nothing like it.

Edith (*correcting her*) You never felt anything like it.

Anna You never felt anything like it.

Edith That's better.

Letty Well, I'll just see that Arthur's got everything. He'll want some fresh coffee making.

Anna I'll go, ma'am.

Letty No, Anna, you're wanted here.

Letty picks up the coffee tray and goes off with it towards the kitchen

Edith I began to be quite anxious. I am responsible for you now, Anna, and should you come to any harm I should never forgive myself. You do *see*, don't you?

Anna I see *that*, ma'am. But what I don't see, is what harm could come to me at the fair where everyone's happy enjoying themselves.

Edith That's because you're too young yet to realize what lies beneath the surface of things. Now tell me, that young man—he was a stranger until tonight?

Anna Yes, ma'am.

Edith Yet I suppose you told him your name and everything about yourself?

Anna He asked me.

Edith But he didn't tell you his, I warrant.

Anna (*excitedly*) Yes, he did, ma'am. He did.

Edith Oh? Then what is it?

Anna It's Charles Bradford, ma'am, and he's from London and he's asked me if he can see me again, ma'am.

Edith When?

Anna Tomorrow, ma'am.

Edith Yes—well, that is something we shall have to go into. You may sit down, Anna.

Anna Thank you, ma'am. (*She sits, looking uncomfortable*)

Edith How much have you told him—about yourself, I mean? About your situation?

Anna I told him about the village, ma'am, and how it was you sent for me to come here when my auntie died. And I told him you were the kindest lady I ever knew and the one true friend I had in all the world.

Edith It's really of no concern to anyone, Anna, but how did you come to strike up an acquaintance with this Mr—Bradford, is it—in the first place?

Anna I never did such a thing, ma'am. He struck up with me. Wherever the horses stopped, he was always there waiting.

Edith And you allowed him to pay for you to go on again?

Anna Well, it seemed—it was such a lovely ride, ma'am.

Edith Yes, yes, I dare say, Anna, but to be obliged to a stranger . . .

Anna Oh, I couldn't call him a stranger, ma'am, not now.

Edith Did he walk with you from the Square as far as the house?

Anna He asked to see me home.

Edith He took your arm?

Anna Going across the cobbles, yes, ma'am.

Edith And then—when he said good night—did he—did he make other advances?

Anna Advances, ma'am?

Edith Did he try to kiss you, child?

Anna Oh, well—he said if I didn't *mind* . . .

Edith And you?

Anna He said it wouldn't do me no harm and . . .

Edith It wouldn't do me *any* harm.

Anna It wouldn't do me any harm, he said, and him a great deal of good.

Edith And so you allowed him to kiss you, Anna?

Anna Yes, ma'am.

Edith On the mouth?

Anna (*innocently*) Oh, yes. It was a real, proper kiss, ma'am.

Edith A young man you'd only just set eyes on?

Anna Well, *he'd* only just set eyes on *me*. Besides, his manner and the way he spoke, you could tell he wasn't just anybody. (*Pause*) Couldn't you, ma'am?

Edith (*taken aback*) Well—he seems quite respectable, I must admit, but . . .

Anna Did he smile at you, ma'am?

Edith He seems to have a certain charm, undoubtedly, but . . .

Anna And his eyes—did you look into his eyes, ma'am?

Edith I would agree his eyes are very pleasing, but do you seriously imagine a country-bred girl like you, Anna, who never lived in a town until a month ago, would be sharp enough to capture a young Londoner like him?

Anna I didn't try to capture him, ma'am. I didn't do anything. Besides, he likes country girls better than town girls. He told me so.

Edith You'd hardly expect him to tell you otherwise, would you?

Anna But he truly meant it, ma'am. You could see. (*Pleading*) Oh, ma'am!
(*She rises and moves to Edith*) He has to go back to London the day after
tomorrow.

Edith Then isn't it rather foolish to try to further an acquaintance which
must end so soon in any case?

Anna But it may not, ma'am, for he often has to be down in these parts.

Edith Oh? Has he friends or relatives hereabouts?

Anna Business, I think.

Edith What kind of business?

Anna I don't know, ma'am. I didn't ask him that. But I did say tomorrow
being my regular afternoon off, ma'am, you were always so kind I was
sure it would be all right.

Edith I *try* to be kind, Anna, of course. We all try to be *kind*. But the important thing is to be sure we do what is best.

Anna Who for, ma'am?

Edith Why, for everybody, of course.

*Letty enters with a tray bearing a coffee-pot and a single cup and saucer.
These she sets down, on the sofa table*

Letty (*to Edith*) Arthur says he'll have his coffee in here, Edith.

Edith Oh. Well, then off you go, Anna.

Anna But, ma'am, you haven't said about tomorrow.

Edith Tomorrow, Anna, the fair will be gone and with it all the excitement. It'll be just another ordinary day. Now, don't you think the
sensible thing would be to put this Mr Bradford out of your head?

Anna But I couldn't ma'am. And I shouldn't want to either. Oh, no, I
couldn't do that.

Edith Well, of course you could. It was no more than a chance encounter,
and if I hadn't allowed you to go across to the fair it would never have
happened, would it?

Anna But it has happened, ma'am. And somehow it's made everything
seem—different. Oh, please, ma'am, please! (*She crouches by Edith
imploringly*)

Letty goes to the drinks cupboard and takes out a decanter of brandy

Edith Anna, I am not going to be stampeded into making a foolish
decision. No, off you go, and by the morning I shall have made up my
mind one way or the other.

Letty hands the decanter to Anna

Letty Take Mr Harnham the brandy, Anna.

Anna Yes, ma'am. (*She takes the decanter from Letty and is about to move
off when she suddenly turns to face Edith*) One thing, I can say—Mr
Charles Bradford's a born and bred gentleman to his finger-tips.

Edith (*coldly*) Good night, Anna.

Anna is about to reply, thinks better of it, turns and goes off into the dining-room

Letty The young man wants to see her again, I gather?

Edith Poor Anna! Oh, dear! What the young have to go through, I know exactly how she feels, Letty—exactly.

Letty (*with surprise*) *Do* you, Edith?

Edith Oh, I went through it all when I was her age, and I expect you did, too. One was flattered even to be noticed.

Letty So Anna's not to see him again?

Edith I should love to have said "yes" to the child, Letty, because nobody wants to nip a young affection in the bud, do they? But the circumstances are so—so unusual. Can you imagine what possible attraction a simple girl like Anna would have for a young man-of-the-world such as he?

Letty (*with a laugh*) Really, Edith! That's not a difficult question to answer, surely.

Arthur (*off*) Now off you go to bed. Don't think any more about it . . .

Arthur enters from the dining-room carrying brandy in a goblet

Letty pours his coffee

What's going on, Edith? What's the trouble?

Edith How do you mean, Arthur?

Arthur I gather you've told that girl she's not to be allowed to see her young man tomorrow. On her afternoon off? Is that right?

Edith He's not her young man, Arthur.

Arthur Well, she thinks he is—she was blubbing her eyes out.

Edith They only met for the first time this evening.

Arthur Still, I suppose everybody has to make a start at some point, haven't they?

Edith Anna's being rather tiresome because, in fact, I haven't said one thing or the other.

Arthur Then she must have got hold of the wrong end of the stick. Anyhow, she's all right now, as right as rain and gone up to bed smiling. (*He moves to the niche and from one of the lower shelves takes a Halma board on which a half-finished game is already set out*) Here we are, that's right.

Sarah enters with an oil lamp. She puts it on the sofa table and goes

We've still last night's game to finish, haven't we? And it was your turn, Edith, when we left off. (*He puts the board down on a low table in front of Edith*) There! Take your time, now. I can see a splendid move waiting for you. Don't miss it.

Edith When you say Anna's right as rain now, Arthur, what do you mean exactly?

Arthur Oh, I told her not to worry, of course.

Edith About what?

Arthur About tomorrow. I told her it would be all right.

Edith Do you mean you told her she could see this man again?

Arthur Certainly. After all, how she likes to spend her afternoons off is her affair, isn't it?

Edith But, Arthur, I feel a personal responsibility for this girl.

Arthur Not for her private life. That's no concern of ours.

Edith It would be—if she should get into trouble.

Arthur For God's sake, Edith! Anna's a servant-girl—nothing more. And we've had a great many in and out of this house in the last twenty years. They know damn well that if they're unlucky enough to get themselves lumbered, then out they go. In any case, the fellows either pay up or marry 'em in the end.

Edith Not always.

Arthur Anyhow, let's get on with our game.

Edith No, Arthur. I'm sorry. If you don't mind, I won't play tonight, I—I don't feel I could concentrate. Good night, Letty.

Letty Oh—good night, Edith.

Edith goes off up the stairs

There is a short silence during which Arthur is inwardly seething. At the same time, he has his eye on Letty, watching for her reaction, but she continues with her needlework, refusing to catch his eye

Arthur Well? I did the wrong thing, I suppose?

Letty Unless you intended to upset her, Arthur.

Arthur Just because I told the girl she can please herself what she does on her afternoons off—what is there upsetting about that?

Letty Arthur, please. Don't go on about it. There's nothing to be gained, is there? Here—come along—I'll play Edith's corner for her.

Arthur All right.

Letty lays aside her needlework and sits at the Halma board

It's your move.

Letty at once moves a piece. There is a pause as both study the board, but Arthur is not thinking of the game

All the same, I sometimes wonder, if I hadn't come along when I did, what would have become of Edith.

Letty Oh, I wouldn't have said you were the only pebble on the beach.

Arthur They hadn't a penny, you know, not a penny.

Letty If you hadn't come along the answer's quite simple. She'd have married someone else.

Arthur At her age? With that old father to nurse? Besides, in that God-forsaken village she hardly saw a new face from one year's end to another. If I hadn't driven over that day to look at a few acres of barley . . .

Letty Really, it's not a bit of good talking to me like that, Arthur, because

I *know*. From the first moment you set eyes on her, you made all the running. Think of all the times you had me chasing up mutual friends—arranging things so that the pair of you would meet.

Arthur (*moving a piece on the board*) Yes, you played the match-maker rather well.

Letty I simply tried to be helpful. To my mind, you've been extremely lucky. You're disappointed, of course, at not having a son, but you've only been married three years—Edith's still a young woman. And how hard she's tried to make a success of everything.

Arthur And haven't I? She's a comfortable home here, a very generous allowance. She's free to come and go as she likes, she gets a damn sight more out of life *here* than she ever did in that village.

Letty You don't understand. She was needed there, Arthur.

Letty is about to continue, but Arthur silences her

Sarah enters with a second lighted oil-lamp which she places on the hall table, and then moves to the windows to draw the curtains. For a moment she stands agape, captivated by the bright lights of the fair, until Arthur's voice brings her back to earth

Arthur It's your move.

With a shrug, Letty resumes her game as Sarah begins to untie the curtains, and—

the CURTAIN *falls*

SCENE 2

The same. A sunny morning ten days later

As the CURTAIN *rises, Sarah, pursued by Anna, darts into the room from the hall with a letter in her hand. To avoid surrendering it, she jumps up on the seat of a chair, holding the letter high above her head, while Anna tries vainly to reach it. Both girls are wearing their morning print dresses and their caps and aprons. Brooms and a box of cleaning gear are visible in the hall*

Sarah Who's it from? Who's it from?

Anna Oh, Sarah! Give it me! Give it me!

Sarah Who's it from? Who's it from?

Anna How can I tell you who it's from till I read it, you stupid. Oh, do give it me—*please*, Sarah.

With difficulty, because of Anna's clutching hands, Sarah reads out the super-scription

Sarah "Miss Anna Dunsford, at The Brewer's House, Market Square,

Salisbury, Wiltshire." I know who it's from!

Anna You do not.

Sarah Yes, I do. Posted in London, it's from that feller.

Anna What feller.

Sarah *What* feller? My! Aren't you cool! Why the feller at the fair, of course, what walked you out the earthworks Old Sarum way.

Anna It's not him, Sarah, no—truly it isn't. Oh, give it me. Go on, give it me.

Sarah (*teasing*) I don't suppose you ever had a letter from a feller before, did you?

Anna No—because I never had a feller before, that's why.

Sarah You wait till you've been walking out as long as me and Bertie have.

Letty enters downstairs. She is dressed for a routine visit to the local shops and carries a basket

Letty Sarah! Come down off the furniture! What *are* you doing?

Sarah quickly jumps down from the chair and thrusts the letter into Anna's hands

Sarah Nothing, ma'am.

Letty Nothing?

Sarah No, ma'am.

Letty Well, you can't do much less than nothing, can you? The point is you should be at your work at this time of the morning, not larking about. What is it you have there, Anna?

Anna It's a letter, ma'am.

Letty I can see it's a letter, you silly girl. But who's it for?

Anna It's for me, ma'am.

Letty Oh? Let me look.

Reluctantly, Anna holds out the envelope so that Letty is able to read the face of it

Hmm! So it is. Well? Aren't you going to open it?

Anna I don't want to open it, not yet, ma'am, if you'll excuse me. (*She stuffs the letter into the front of her dress*) I just want to keep it a bit.

Letty You funny girl! (*To Sarah*) Don't stand there with your mouth open, child. Now, get along, both of you. You should be quite finished downstairs by this time.

Sarah So we are, ma'am. Come on, Anna.

Sarah goes off into the hallway, picks up the box of cleaning-gear and, followed by Anna with brooms and dusters, is about to climb the stairs as Edith starts to descend. Both girls wait side by side at the foot of the stairs until their mistress passes them

Edith Good morning, Sarah—Anna.

Sarah ⎫
Anna ⎭ *(bobbing)* Good morning, ma'am.

Edith comes down to Letty, two lending-library books in her hand as the two girls hurry off up the stairs. She gives the books to Letty who puts them into her shopping-basket

Edith If you can catch Miss Stevens, she knows what I like. *(Moving to her desk)* Oh—and I've a small shopping list here for you, Letty—just a few odds and ends I need from Bowden's, if you wouldn't mind. And Arthur specially asked me to remind you to speak about the bacon. He said it was dreadfully salt again this morning.

Letty I didn't find it salty in the least. Did you?

Edith No.

Letty No! I suspect Arthur's just being rather faddy.

Edith He was so grumpy at breakfast, I began to wonder if it was something I'd said or done.

Letty I know exactly what it is. Yesterday, you see, Tremlett's turned down the offer from our firm. Didn't he tell you?

Edith No.

Letty Oh! Oh well, of course, he doesn't want you to have the worry.

Edith Sometimes he makes me feel so inadequate.

Letty My dear Edith, Arthur thinks the world of you. He's always telling me so.

Edith He doesn't tell me.

Letty Ah, but he wouldn't. That's not his way. *(She picks up her basket)* Now, there's nothing else, is there? I may be some little time because I have to visit two of our work-people. There's one old dear of ninety-seven who still talks about Waterloo as if it were yesterday.

Edith Oh, then you must let me give you something, Letty.

Edith opens one of the drawers of the desk, takes out a small cash-box and from it a silver coin

Letty Oh, there's really no need, Edith.

Edith But I'd like to. I insist. There! Now, you buy them both a box of those nice meat cubes.

Letty *(accepting the money)* Well, thank you, Edith. They *will* appreciate it. It *is* so kind of you.

Edith *(sitting at her desk)* Oh, nonsense! The truth is one can do so little.

Letty It won't seem little to them, Edith. That's why the poor are so useful. One can always help them without being unduly extravagant.

Letty goes off towards the front door

Edith prepares to attend to her correspondence

Anna appears on the stairs, where she pauses until the front door has closed behind Letty. She then comes quickly down and into the room

For a moment Edith remains unaware of her presence

Anna Oh, ma'am.
Edith (*turning in her chair*) Yes, Anna? What is it?
Anna (*fumbling in her dress*) I've had a letter come, ma'am.
Edith Well?
Anna (*producing the now opened envelope*) The trouble is—I can't read a single word in it.
Edith But of course you can. You've been getting on so well with your reading.
Anna But I can't, ma'am. You see, it's all in handwriting.
Edith Then you'd better ask Cook to read it to you when she has time.
Anna But this is from somebody—I don't want just anyone to read it, ma'am.
Edith (*suddenly curious*) Is it from that young man?
Anna I think so, ma'am.
Edith Why, then I'll read it to you, child. You needn't worry, I shan't say a word to anyone.

Reluctantly, Anna takes the letter from its envelope and hands it to Edith

Anna (*fearfully*) Oh, ma'am!
Edith What is it?
Anna I think it's you knowing, ma'am—things so—so private.
Edith (*offering to return the letter*) Well, if you feel that way about it then I *shan't* read it.
Anna (*desperately*) But I must know what he says, ma'am.
Edith You can't have it both ways, Anna. If you think it'll make you feel shy and bashful then go and stare out of the window while I read it out to you.
Anna Yes, ma'am.

Anna moves up stage of Edith and faces the window

Edith (*unfolding the letter*) Are you quite ready?
Anna (*trembling*) Yes, ma'am.

Edith reads the letter in a flat, hard, matter-of-fact voice

Edith (*reading*) A hundred and seventy-four, Gray's Inn Road, London, Tuesday. Dearest, why—oh, why have you not written? Did we not agree that you were to write first? Just imagine—for ten nights now I have lain awake trying to recapture the exact look of your sweet face as I first saw it that evening at the fair, sometimes succeeding, sometimes not, but always praying that tomorrow will bring me word from you until, as you see, I can wait no longer. I do so need you to tell me that what I believe to exist between us is true and not the wild imagining of a mind bewitched. To love vainly can be a torment, but to love and to know that one is loved in return is to breathe the very air of heaven. Do, therefore, dearest, write as soon as you are able and restore me to a more tolerable state of mind. For ever, C.B.

There is a pause. Edith looks at the letter again, then folds it up

Anna (*turning from the window*) Thank you, ma'am.

Edith Were you quite able to follow it all?

Anna (*doubtfully*) Yes, I think so, ma'am. It doesn't really say much, does it? (*More cheerfully*) But it's a lovely letter, though.

Edith (*dryly*) I should call it a remarkable letter. Considering that you've met only twice before, it could scarcely go much further.

Anna What I meant was, it doesn't say when he's next coming down this way, or if we're ever going to see each other again, or—or anything.

Edith Well, that'll be something for you to write about when you come to reply, won't it? (*She hands the letter to Anna*)

Anna (*anxiously*) Oh, you'll do that for me, ma'am, won't you?

Edith I?

Anna Please, ma'am, because I couldn't bear him to think I'm not able to do it myself. I'd sink into the earth with shame if he knew that.

Edith But you know all your letters now, Anna. At least, you can print them.

Anna That's not the same, ma'am. I mean, it's not real writing, is it? And whatever would he think of me?

Edith It so happens I was looking through your copy-book only this morning. (*She takes a school copy-book from the drawer of the desk*) I have it here. Now look how far you've come since we first did these hooks and hangers together, haven't you?

Anna Yes, ma'am, but . . .

Edith (*turning the pages*) And there! You see, you can write quite well when you put your mind to it. And here—look—you've written whole words together. (*Reading*) "Patience and Perseverance brought the snail to Jerusalem."

Anna That's only copying, ma'am. I couldn't do it, not without something to go by. Anyway, it just looks like it was done by some little maid at school.

Edith You're still only a girl, Anna. (*She replaces the copy-book*)

Anna I'm a woman, ma'am—now.

There is a pause. Edith turns in her chair to look Anna full in the face. Anna boldly returns the stare. Edith drops her eyes

Edith (*taking back the letter*) There was something in the letter I didn't quite . . . (*Reading*) "I do so need you to tell me that what I believe to exist between us is true . . ." What does he believe? What do you take that to mean, Anna?

Anna It means he believes we love each other, ma'am.

Edith And do *you* believe that?

Anna Yes, ma'am.

There is a pause. Edith rises from the desk and moves away from the desk, the letter still in her hand, then turns and faces Anna

Anna watches her anxiously

Edith If I'm to help you with your letter, Anna—and I say *if* because I'm not at all sure it's the right and proper thing to do—but if I am to help you, then I must know—certain things. Now you do see that, don't you?

Anna Yes, ma'am.

Edith Now—on the day after the fair, when you had the afternoon off, this young man, this Mr Bradford, he hired a fly, didn't he, to drive you both out to the edge of the plain?

Anna To see the old earthworks.

Edith (*dryly*) Yes—well, I don't suppose your afternoon was spent discussing archaeology.

Anna We found ourselves a nice grassy little hollow in the sun and out of the way of the wind. And there we stopped till it was time for me to be getting back.

Edith (*uneasily*) I see. And you—you talked, I suppose.

Anna Some of the time, ma'am.

Edith About your future? I mean, did you come to any sort of understanding?

Anna Not the sort you could put into words, ma'am. Most of the time we just lay there.

Edith (*sharply*) Kissing and cuddling?

Anna does not answer

You remember that Betsy Hartnell in the village and the nasty things they used to say about *her*?

Anna I do, ma'am. But they do say, don't they, that a girl can sometimes be that hungry she don't always wait for the parson to say grace. Besides, there was plenty of girls went on worse than Betsy Hartnell and did better. And they always say you're unlucky to g et caught first time, don't they, ma'am?

Edith (*disturbed*) Do they? I don't know, Anna. I don't know what they say. But one thing's quite clear—you've surrendered yourself body and soul to a man of whom you know nothing and after only the briefest acquaintance.

Anna I couldn't have done no other, ma'am. It would have gone against nature.

Edith But to commit the whole of your future happiness to the outcome of what may be only a passing attachment . . . Oh, Anna!

Anna If it was only that, he'd no need to write.

Edith He lives in London, remember, a hundred miles from here, Anna, with—theatres, concerts, dinner-parties—and there he has his friends, his occupation and, I dare say, countless other distractions as well. You may not see him again for weeks on end. Do you think his interest in you is going to survive all that?

Anna (*agitated*) Oh, I do feel so. It must do. And if you help me then it surely will. Please ma'am . . .

Edith Wait now, Anna. Sit down. Just let us consider. To ignore the letter, if you could being yourself to do such a thing, would make you utterly miserable, wouldn't it?

Anna Yes, it would so, ma'am.

Edith On the other hand, I agree that for me to leave you to write on your own as best you can might not, at this stage, produce the happiest result.

Anna No, it would not, ma'am.

Edith So I really have no alternative, have I? Very well then, Anna. I'll try to help you as far as I can.

Anna (*fervently*) Oh, thank you, ma'am. And shall we write it now while Miss Harnham's still out at the shop?

Edith But what about your duties, Anna? (*Moving to her desk*) What are they this morning?

Anna Only the front bedroom, ma'am, sweeping and dusting. It had its proper turn-out yesterday.

Edith But have you had time to think out just what you want to say?

Anna Oh, I know what to say, ma'am, if only you'll put it for me.

Edith (*sitting at her desk*) Well, then let us begin. It'd be sensible, I think, not to use my writing-paper. We'll use this plain scribbling-block which is just the sort of thing you might have yourself. Now—(*She takes up a pen*)—the address and the date, of course. What do you call your Mr Bradford?

Anna Charles, ma'am.

Edith Charles, I see. Then shall we begin "My dear Charles" or "Dearest Charles" or just simply "Dear Charles"?

Anna I don't like none of those, ma'am.

Edith (*needled*) I don't like *any* of those, you should say.

Anna I don't like any of those. You see, what I want is for him to feel that I'm actually there right close beside him, ma'am.

Edith (*coldly*) Then what do you suggest?

Anna I'd like to start off "To my own true love, my very dearest, most precious sweetheart."

Edith puts down her pen

Edith No, no, Anna. That is *not* the way to begin a letter.

Anna Why isn't it, ma'am?

Edith Because it's both so wildly extravagant and so clumsy. Letter-writing, you see, is hung about with certain conventions, which simply must be observed, and I'm sure Mr Bradford would expect you to have some knowledge of them however slight. The aim is to be simple, truthful and unaffected. Extravagance of any kind is always vulgar. Now you do see that, don't you?

Anna (*doubtfully*) Well—yes, ma'am.

Edith In his letter to you, he begins very simply, "Dearest". Just the one superlative. Quite enough. No one wants to be so smothered by words at the outset that there is nothing further to be said, let alone hinted at. And there's another thing to remember, too, although it may not always be the case, but a gentleman likes to imagine he is pursuing the young lady and *not* the other way about. (*She picks up the pen*) So—let us begin again.

Anna Then it'd better be just "Dear Charles", ma'am.

Edith No one could find fault with that, Anna. Although the warmth of his own letter is such that you could afford to be a little more responsive. I think if I were writing for myself, which of course I'm not, I should begin—"Beloved". Just that—"Beloved".

Anna (*dismally*) "Beloved", ma'am?

Edith Yes. I find it a tender, comforting word, Anna. It's a word that can be used without losing one's self-possession. One can retain a certain dignity, and still say so much. Yes, that's the word *I* would choose—"Beloved".

Anna But I've heard them using that word in church, ma'am.

Edith I've no doubt you have. Love comes into everything, Anna.

Anna Well, if you think it *says* enough, ma'am, and you think it's *right*, then I'll be guided by you.

Edith Good. Now—"Why—oh, why have you not written?" he asks. Yes—well, we know very well why, don't we?

Anna But I don't want *him* to know, ma'am.

Edith Nevertheless, always answer questions, Anna. Nothing annoys a correspondent more than to have his queries ignored. But what is it you wish to say first?

Anna Ooh—say how worried I was, ma'am, not hearing, and what a blessed relief it was when his letter come this morning.

Edith (*as she writes*) Came this morning, Anna—*came*.

Anna Came this morning. And . . .

Edith Now—to the question why you haven't written before the answer is, no matter what arrangement you may have agreed to, it was surely his place to write first.

Anna But I would have written the very next day, ma'am, if I'd been able to.

Edith Possibly. However, as things have turned out, I feel it's just as well you didn't.

Anna But I wouldn't like him to think I didn't write because I didn't care one way or the other.

Edith He won't get that impression.

There is a pause. Anna peers anxiously over Edith's shoulder as the letter continues to write

The fact that, after time for reflection, he's stated his feelings so positively puts us on much firmer ground, Anna.

Anna Then I can say how much I love him, can I, ma'am?

Edith The whole letter is saying that, Anna.

Anna Then say would he write soon and tell me when he'll be down this way next, ma'am.

There is a pause. Edith continues writing

If I knew exactly when we'd see each other again the waiting wouldn't be so bad.

Another pause. Edith goes on writing

It's when you can't see an end to waiting, that's what makes the days seem long.

Another pause

And say I think of him all the time, ma'am—every blessed minute of the day.

Finally, Edith lays down her pen and takes up the letter

Edith There! Now, I'll read it through to you, Anna, and if there's anything you don't like you must say so.
Anna Yes, ma'am. (*She sits*)

Anna shuts her eyes, clasps her hands up to her mouth and sits rigid. Edith reads carefully, modulating each phrase in an effort to make the meaning clear to Anna

Edith (*reading*) "Beloved, your letter arrived this morning like a burst of sunlight and turned my foolish fears and anxieties to happiness and relief. Despite our arrangement, I hesitated to write myself in case you had found on your return to London that the sentiments you had expressed were less deeply felt than you supposed. (*She rises and moves to Anna*) A letter from me would then have been little more than a tiresome reminder of a chance encounter best forgotten. Although I am more than happy to learn that my fears are groundless, I live now only for the moment of our next meeting. I hope you will write soon and tell me when we can hope to see each other again. You are always in my thoughts—Anna."
Anna (*after a pause*) It's beautiful, ma'am, just beautiful. I couldn't for the life of me have made that up out of my own head, but now you've written it down I feel it exactly.
Edith Then won't you, at least, put your name to it? You can write your own name perfectly well.
Anna (*rising*) Oh, no, ma'am! I should do it so bad. He'd be bound to notice at once. And then where should I be?
Edith Very well. (*Sitting at her desk again*) Then you'd like it to go just as it stands?
Anna Yes, please, ma'am. And when you've done the envelope may I slip out and post it in the box myself?
Edith (*selecting an envelope*) Oh, there's no need for that. Just leave it on the hall table. It can go with Mr. Harnham's letters this evening.
Anna Oh, ma'am. You don't understand—I'd like to post it myself, ma'am.
Edith (*addressing the envelope*) It won't get there any quicker.
Anna No, but I've never posted a letter before, not of my own.
Edith (*gently*) Have you not, Anna?
Anna No, ma'am.
Edith Then you shall post this one.
Anna Oh, thank you, ma'am.
Edith *If* I have a stamp. (*She searches*) Yes, I have. (*She affixes the stamp*

and thumps it with her fist) There!

Edith hands the letter to Anna who kisses it and is ready to fly

You may slip out the front way, if you wish, but put your cloak on,
mind, to go into the street.
Anna Yes, ma'am. I'll fetch it, ma'am. Thank you, ma'am.

*Clutching the letter, Anna hurries out and goes off towards the back of
the house to find her cloak*

*Edith starts to tidy her desk. Presently, she picks up Mr Bradford's letter.
She studies it for a moment. Overcome by a mixture of self-pity and genuine
desire, she is unable to continue and puts it down*

*At this point, Anna, her cloak flying, runs down the hall towards the front
door which can be heard to open.*

Arthur (*off*) Careful, girl! Careful now! Look where you're going!
Anna (*off*) Sorry, sir. Beg pardon, sir.
Arthur (*off*) I should think so. I should think so.

*The front door is heard to close. At the sound of Arthur's voice, Edith is
thrown into a confusion of guilt. She quickly thrusts Mr Bradford's letter into
a drawer of the desk and closes it, rising and picking up her sewing basket*

Arthur enters from the hall

Arthur Where the devil's that girl off to at this hour, Edith?
Edith (*recovering her composure*) Anna? Oh, she's just slipped out to post
a letter for me, Arthur.

The Lights fade as—

the CURTAIN *falls*

SCENE 3

The same. A Sunday evening, some six weeks later

As the CURTAIN *rises, Arthur enters from the study with some papers. As
Letty speaks he listens, then goes to pour himself a sherry*

Letty (*off*) No, no no! I have been to a Choral Eucharist, Edith. I didn't
like it at all. It seemed to have so very little to do with the Last Supper.

Edith and Letty appear in the hall. Edith notes Arthur going to the drinks

Edith Quite. And that's exactly why poor Father always tried to strike a balance.

Letty I'm sure he did, dear. Well, I shall go and take off my hat.

Letty exits upstairs

Edith, carrying her prayer-book and hymn-book, both bound in ivory, moves to the bell-pull

Edith It *was* Canon Rawsley, Arthur. I said it would be. And what a magnificent sermon! I do wish you'd heard it. (*She pulls the bell-rope*)

The sound of the bell is heard off

Arthur Yes.

Edith I found it most upsetting, and I'm sure Letty did, too.

Arthur Oh? What was he on about?

Edith He was describing the dreadful conditions that exist among the poor in the East End of London. Do you know, Arthur, he told us of finding the little bodies of newly born babies thrown out on to the rubbish heaps. And these things are *true*, Arthur. Canon Rawsley actually lives and works amongst it all. It made me feel so ashamed.

Arthur What have you to be ashamed of?

Edith I do so little.

Arthur Nonsense!

Edith It isn't nonsense, Arthur. How *can* one turn one's back on so much poverty and misery?

Sarah enters

Edith Oh, Sarah, please tell Anna I'd like to see her.

Sarah Anna's not back yet, ma'am.

Edith Not back yet! She's very late. Then remember to tell her as soon as she comes in.

Sarah Very well, ma'am.

Arthur (*patiently*) My dear Edith, this world is as it is. There's bound to be inequality. I was talking to our member of Parliament only last night, and he actually expressed the view that poverty is an economic necessity.

Edith Then he should have been there this evening to hear Canon Rawsley.

Arthur Well, of course, Rawsley is obliged to lay it on pretty thick to get people to dig into their pockets, isn't he? But why stay on for the sermon if it upsets you so?

Edith A good sermon is meant to upset one.

Arthur (*amused*) What you mean is you thoroughly enjoyed it. Worth every penny of half a sovereign, I've no doubt. (*He sits on the sofa to read his documents*)

Edith I didn't have half a sovereign in my purse unfortunately—only half a crown. But then when he spoke of the terrible drunkenness that prevails—the men like animals and the women even worse—I couldn't help thinking that we share some of the responsibility. You and I, Arthur!

Arthur Eh? You mean on account of the brewery? But our beers don't reach the London market. I wish they did.

Edith But it's the same trade, Arthur, and our comfortable lives depend on it.

Arthur (*sharply*) Brewing is something more than a trade, Edith. (*Exploding*) Good heavens! I've been into this I don't know how many times. Anything can be abused. Some people drink too much—yes—and other people eat too much. But you don't suggest farmers should stop growing food because of that, do you?

Edith I'm sorry, Arthur. I only meant . . .

Arthur (*rising and facing Edith*) What do you suppose we should do? Give up and leave the whole field clear for Tremlett? What would happen to our work-people? Some have been with us ever since Father's time. Who'll look after them if we go?

Edith Well—no, I see that you can't just . . .

Arthur You're quite right, you can't. Nowadays, in my opinion, there are far too many people about trying to do good. Good means don't necessarily lead to good ends, you know. (*He sits*) Consequently, when they leave off the sum total of human misery is nearly always far greater than when they began. Take my advice, Edith—*be* good, if you can, but for heaven's sake don't start trying to *do* good. Leave that to the Almighty.

Edith But how else can God work except through us, His creatures? After all, we're only here to do His will, aren't we?

Arthur Yes, but the difficulty is to be sure it's God's will and not the other feller's.

Letty, who has taken off her hat, enters from the stairs

Letty Edith, Anna's just back. I saw them from my window and I *thought* I heard Mansell shouting something about an accident . . .

Edith (*alarmed*) An accident? Is Anna all right? What happened?

Letty I don't know what happened, Edith. As for Anna, she jumped down from the trap looking as right as a trivet. It can't have been anything serious.

Edith All the same, I'll just go and find out. (*As she goes*) Something must have happened or they wouldn't have been so late.

Edith hurries off

Arthur (*rising and collecting his sherry and documents*) You'd think the whole world revolved round that wretched girl. I tell you, Letty, I've a damned good mind to send her home for good. (*He moves towards the study*)

Letty Edith would be terribly upset if you did.

Arthur (*turning*) She'd get over it. Something must be done. It's becoming quite absurd.

Letty I see no point in sending the girl away now. I'm surprised you even suggest it.

Arthur Oh? Why?

Letty Because there's been such a difference in Edith these last few weeks.

Arthur In what way?

Letty She's happy, Arthur.

Arthur Happy?

Letty Yes, I'd say Edith's happier now than at any time since I've known her.

Arthur Would you!

Letty Oh, *yes*! She looks younger, too, and she's so full of life and high spirits.

Arthur Are you telling me now, then, that Edith's happiness is determined by this chit of a servant girl?

Letty No, no, of course I'm not. No, Arthur, I'd hoped this difference in Edith was because—well—because things between you both were—better.

Arthur (*drily*) Did you? Well, all I can tell you is that in these last few weeks Edith has seemed to me even more distant than usual. I'll not say any more.

Letty Oh. Well, there must *be* a reason. (*With a sigh*) Oh, dear! Women *are* such complicated creatures. Perhaps you're just beginning to find that out.

Arthur It may surprise you, Letty, but I learnt a fair bit about women long before I met Edith, you know.

Letty Well, of course. I'm not saying . . .

Arthur And I didn't take my lessons in the drawing-room, either. Does that shock you?

Letty I—I don't think so.

Arthur I only mention it so you'll understand that I do know when a relationship is working satisfactorily and when it is not.

Edith enters quickly, having taken off her hat

Edith Would you believe it? They'd only just set out when a pheasant started up right under the horse's feet. They went over into the ditch and broke a wheel. Poor Mansell had to walk back for another.

Arthur Nobody was hurt, I gather.

Edith Anna's looking rather pale, but Mansell's tucking into a plateful of cold beef and pickles, so I imagine it was only a shaking.

Letty Do you know what he's brought, Edith?

Edith Yes. New potatoes, broad beans, lettuce and spring onions.

Letty I'll go and settle up with him. He won't go until he gets his money.

Letty exits towards the rear of the house

Edith sits at her desk. She opens a drawer to check that Charles's letters are there, then closes it

Edith (*as she moves*) Of course, Anna's only to be away from here for a night and a day to come back speaking almost as broadly as ever she did. It's really quite disheartening.

Arthur But hardly surprising, Edith.

Edith How do you mean?

Arthur I don't imagine she'd be encouraged to show off her airs and graces among her own people, would she?

Edith Why do you accuse her of putting on airs and graces, Arthur, just because she wants to learn how to speak properly?

Arthur I expect you think I'm stuffy and old-fashioned. But you see, to me a good servant is just as valuable as a good master. Try to turn one into the other and you lose both.

Edith Not always. And why *should* a girl have to miss the finer opportunities of life just because she doesn't know how to make the best of herself?

Arthur Give her the chance, Edith, and she'll make her own opportunities. As it is, you're letting the girl and her affairs fill your entire life.

Edith No more than the brewery fills yours.

Arthur But brewing is my vocation, Edith. It's something I care about. And when I think of Father and Grandfather and great-Grandfather before that, I should feel ashamed if I *didn't* care. We all owe something to the past as well as to the future, don't we? Can't you see that? (*Pause*) A glass of sherry?

Edith (*miserably*) No, thank you, Arthur.

There is another pause

Arthur Edith I . . . Don't think I'm reproaching you. But things were not —well—like this between us at the beginning, were they? (*Pause*) What's happened?

Edith Nothing's happened, Arthur. It's just that . . .

Arthur You see, if I didn't know that such a thing was inconceivable, I could so easily jump to quite the wrong conclusion.

Edith I don't know what you mean.

Arthur I might easily imagine from the way you're behaving that—some-one has come between us.

Edith (*with a nervous laugh*) Arthur, you're being quite absurd. Really, that's ridiculous. And—it's not worthy of you.

Anna appears

(*Suddenly and gratefully aware of her*) Yes, Anna?

Anna My brother-in-law's just set off home, ma'am, and he said I was to say thank you for his supper which he much enjoyed.

Edith Thank you, Anna.

Anna (*with a glance at Arthur*) Shall I come back when it's more convenient, ma'am? Only you did say that as soon as . . .

Anna breaks off. Highly irritated by the interruption, Arthur strides towards his study

Arthur (*as he moves*) We'll talk later, Edith.

Ignoring Anna, Arthur goes off into his study, closing the door sharply behind him

Edith You're still looking rather pale. You didn't bang your head on anything, I hope?

Anna No, ma'am. We went over nice and easy and tumbled out quite soft.

Edith Well, did it feel strange to find yourself in the village again?

Anna Oh, ma'am! Everything looks so small.

Edith Then you didn't feel you'd rather be back there again?

Anna Not now, ma'am. I don't ever want to go back there now.

Edith Still, Rose was glad to see you, wasn't she, and hear all your news?

Anna Well, I doubt I'd have had that much of a welcome if you hadn't given me that lovely basket of good things to take, ma'am.

Edith Oh nonsense, Anna.

Anna I don't mean that not in any nasty way, ma'am. It's just that there's not a mouthful to spare. Fifteen shillings a week he gets, and four children to keep.

Edith Poor Rose! It must be a struggle.

Anna She's my only close relation now, ma'am, but she's not the kind I could ever turn to for anything. Life's ever so hard for them.

Edith Did you tell them about your Mr Bradford?

Anna Oh, I couldn't hold it back, ma'am—not with Wednesday so close now. Besides, all through the day I'm saying to myself, this time on Wednesday he'll be on the train. And then, this time on Wednesday I'll be at the station waiting for him—and then, this time on Wednesday we'll both be together again. So I had to speak about him, ma'am.

Edith Anna—after you left on Saturday, another letter came for you.

Anna Another letter?

Edith Yes, by the afternoon post. I have answered it for you already.

Anna But—in the last letter he said he wouldn't write again, ma'am, because he'd be here so soon.

Edith Nevertheless. (*She holds out the letter to Anna*)

Anna Would you read it out for me please, ma'am.

Edith Now surely you can read most of it for yourself, Anna, and it's time you began to make the effort. Well, if you like to spell out the long words, I'll tell you how to say them.

Anna (*taking the envelope reluctantly*) Very well, ma'am. (*She takes the letter from its envelope and begins to read*) "Dearest, I am quite . . ." (*She pauses, puzzled by a word*) D-e-s-p-o-n- . . .

Edith Despondent.

Anna (*saying the word*) Despondent.

Edith That's right. What Mr Bradford's trying to tell you, Anna, is just

how wretched and miserable he feels.
Anna But why, ma'am. Why should he?
Edith Well, read on, child, read on and you'll find out.
Anna (*reading slowly*) "It is with a heevy . . ."
Edith Heavy.
Anna "It is with a heavy heart that I find myself obliged to send you the dismal . . ." (*Pause*) I-n-f-o-r-m . . .
Edith Information. Here, give it to me. You're not catching the sense of it at all. (*She takes the letter and begins to read briskly*) "It is with a heavy heart that I find myself obliged to send you the dismal information that circumstances, all unforeseen, have suddenly arisen which make it impossible for me to travel to the West on Wednesday as I had planned."
Anna (*fearfully*) Does it mean he's not coming, ma'am?
Edith It means he's not coming on Wednesday, Anna.
Anna Oh, but I . . .
Edith Wait, wait—see how it goes on: "Will you ever forgive me, I wonder? Will I ever forgive myself? But I can see no opportunity at the moment of my being able to leave London much before the end of next month, so your letters will be all . . ."
Anna (*faintly*) Next month? Oh, ma'am! (*Her knees give way and she sinks to the floor in a faint*)
Edith Anna! Child! What is it?

Edith goes down on her knees beside Anna and begins to slap her on the hand

Oh, there! I said you should have gone straight up to bed the moment you came in, and I should have sent Sarah for Dr Warren.

There is no immediate response from Anna. Edith gets to her feet and starts for the hall then, changing her mind, hurries to the desk. From one of the smaller drawers, she takes a bottle of smelling-salts and returns to the prostrate Anna. Kneeling, she raises the girl's head and holds the smelling-salts under her nose

Anna Oh, ma'am. What . . . ?
Edith You've been in a faint, Anna. Now, take a good sniff at these.

Anna does so, then coughs and splutters

Once again. There—that's better, isn't it? They make the eyes water, but they clear the brain, I'll help you up and you can sit quietly in that chair for a little. Can you manage?
Anna I think so, ma'am.

With Edith's help, Anna gets to her feet and sinks into a nearby chair

Edith You see, I was perfectly right. That accident gave you more of a shock than you imagined. You must go upstairs and get into bed, and in the morning we'll ask Dr Warren to give you a thorough examination.
Anna No, ma'am, no. I—I don't need to see a doctor, ma'am.
Edith But if there's something wrong, Anna?

Anna It's not a doctor I *need*, ma'am, it's Charles.

Edith Oh?

Anna You won't turn me out, ma'am, will you? Please—please say you won't turn me out. Only I can't keep it to myself, not for another whole month, can I?

Edith (*after a pause*) How can you be so sure?

Anna I've had all the signs, ma'am. And Rose, she knows all about *them*.

Towards the rear of the house, the gong is sounded

Edith I hardly know what to say, Anna. Still less what to do!

Arthur emerges from the study and crosses in silence to the dining-room, glaring at Anna in passing.
  Letty comes down the stairs

Letty (*entering*) There's the gong, Edith—oh, you have Anna with you.

Edith Arthur's just gone in, Letty. I shall be along presently. Don't wait for me.

Letty Oh, very well. (*She looks curiously from one to the other*) Is there something the matter?

Edith Anna's not feeling quite herself, but it's nothing serious, we hope.

Letty It might have been serious. You've been very lucky, Anna. Don't be too long, Edith, will you?

Letty goes off into the dining-room

Anna If you was to turn me out now, ma'am, whatever would become of me?

Edith (*sharply*) Don't be stupid, child! There's no question of that at the moment. But quite soon your condition will become increasingly difficult to conceal, and I know very well what Mr Harnham's attitude will be.

Anna But when Charles finds out what's happened to me, he'll stand by me—won't he, ma'am?

Edith (*instinctively*) Stand by you? What do you mean, *marry* you? Oh, but he can't do *that*!

Anna But he must! Why not? Why can't he, ma'am?

Edith Because—well, because that kind of young man—no, no, Anna, it's most improbable.

Anna But he loves me? And he's always saying he loves me.

Edith A man may say many things in the course of a casual acquaintance, Anna, but he can be just as quick to repudiate them the moment he faces any *real* responsibility.

Anna Oh! Then whatever shall I do? Oh, ma'am!

Edith Try not to upset yourself, Anna. What we must decide on is our own course of action as calmly and as rationally as possible. Now, it seems to me that the best we can hope for is that he may be persuaded to make proper financial provision for you.

Anna Oh, he'll do more for me than that, my Charles, ma'am. I know he will.

Edith Yes, well, his letters would lead one to think so, but . . . You see, although we've had quite a number, they tell us so little. Of his family, his situation, his financial position, he's never said a word.

Anna I wouldn't care who he was or what he was, ma'am, so long as he still loved me.

Edith (*pacing about*) Obviously, he'll have to be told sooner or later. What we must decide is whether to say nothing until his visit in a month's time, or whether to inform him by letter immediately.

Anna Oh, I want to tell him now, ma'am. I couldn't wait for another whole month not knowing what his feelings are, could I?

Edith I dare say not. But it won't be an easy letter to write, Anna.

Anna Why, ma'am?

Edith Well, because for one thing, I—I've never known myself what it is to be in your situation.

Anna But you can put yourself in my place, ma'am, like you do. And you do it so truly.

Edith There's another thing. We must remember that our letter will probably reach him at his breakfast-table—hardly the time or place one would choose to make such an intimate disclosure. Oh, dear! These things are so much easier to say than they are to put down on paper.

Anna You don't have to mince words, ma'am. It's me that's having the baby—not him.

Edith I'm quite aware of that, Anna.

Anna He knows what went on between us that day just as well as I do, so you can be as plain-spoken as you like.

Edith I shall see no misunderstandings arise, if that's what you mean.

Anna And say he's to come down at once, ma'am, so we can make our arrangements and settle things, and that way I'll have peace of mind.

Edith But, Anna, if I'm to write convincingly, I'm obliged to write as I feel, and so far I always have done. I shall try to put myself in your place, of course, but to change now would be to become quite a different person, perhaps not at all to Mr Bradford's liking.

Anna But I want him to know I'm worried out of my wits, and I will be until I know what he's going to do.

Edith No, Anna, no. I'm sure that's not the attitude we should adopt. Surely the important thing at this stage is for him not to feel you're going to be a burden on him. You want him to know what's happened, of course you do, but you don't want him to think you a great nuisance, do you, and put him to a lot of inconvenience. Aren't I right?

Anna (*doubtfully*) Well, I don't want to be no more trouble than I need, ma'am, so long as he's not going to try and wriggle out of it.

Edith What we must aim at is to keep his interest alive—the interest he already has for you. So I shall tell him what's happened, and I shall say that he continue to write as tenderly as ever, and if he *could* come in a month's time—well—that'll be time enough to discuss what had better be done.

Anna But not ask for anything, won't he think I don't know my rights, ma'am? Is that saying enough, I mean?

Edith It's what I would say, Anna.

Anna All right, ma'am. I'll do what you think's best. Only you've a nicer way with it all than I should have.

Edith Then off you go up to bed, Anna, and I'll come and read you the letter. (*She moves to her desk*)

Anna Oh, thank you, ma'am. (*She seizes Edith's hand and kisses it*) You've been ever so kind.

Edith (*pulling her hand away and turning her head aside*) That'll do, Anna. I'm only trying to do what's best.

Anna Oh, ma'am, I feel better already just having you knowing. (*Turning back*) When you come to the end of the letter, will you say I love him still very much—please?

Edith Of course, Anna.

Anna exits towards the rear of the house

After a moment's pause, Edith moves thoughtfully to her desk. She opens the writing-pad, takes up her pen, and sits thinking for a moment. Suddenly she drops the pen and buries her face in her hands, her whole body shaking with sobs

Letty enters

Letty Edith—Arthur says if you don't . . . My dear! Whatever's the matter?

Edith (*dabbing her eyes*) It's nothing.

Letty Nothing?

Edith I shall be all right in a moment.

Letty Is it—Arthur?

Edith No, no.

Letty Then that girl. Is it Anna? Something she's said? What is it, Edith?

Edith Letty—don't say a word to Arthur—but—the fact is Anna is going to have a child.

Letty Oh, no! Oh, my dear! Do we know who the father is?

Edith You remember the young man she met at the fair?

Letty Well! No wonder you're upset. And after all you've tried to do for the girl. But you mustn't be, Edith, you mustn't be. They're not worth it, you know. They're simply not worth it.

Edith It's not that. You don't understand. I'm not upset with Anna—I envy her.

Letty Edith!

Edith (*rising and placing both hands on the desk*) I envy her, Letty.

Letty Edith, what *are* you saying?

Edith I wish it had been me.

Letty Oh, I *see*! Of course, I see. You mean you wish it was your child —yours and Arthur's. My poor, dear Edith, of course you do!

Edith hurries from the room and up the stairs

(*Following Edith to the foot of the stairs*) And so it will be. It will be one of these days, Edith, I'm sure it will.

CURTAIN

ACT II

SCENE 1

The same. A Saturday afternoon nearly two weeks later
As the CURTAIN *rises, Sarah enters, wearing a clean afternoon cap and apron, and places a cakestand ready for tea. Edith comes downstairs with a bundle of Charles's letters. As she speaks she goes briskly to her desk and places them in a drawer*

Edith Sarah, when the gentleman arrives you're to show him in here, then come and tell me. I shall be in the dining-room.

Sarah Very well, ma'am.

Edith Oh—and you can make the tea as soon as he arrives.

Sarah Tea for—three, ma'am?

Edith No, Sarah—just for two. Don't wait for me to ring. Bring it in as soon as it's ready.

Letty descends the stairs and enters with some show of eagerness

Sarah Yes, ma'am.

Letty Edith, I've just thought of something else.

Edith That'll do then, Sarah.

Sarah Thank you, ma'am.

Sarah goes off

Edith Yes, Letty?

Letty Won't he be expecting to see Anna?

Edith Oh, he knows she's not here today. He's arranged a meeting with Anna for tomorrow. Indeed, that's why he's chosen to come. It was all in his letter to Arthur.

Letty (*suddenly*) Why, Edith, I've just realized—you've put on your new dress.

Edith (*priming a little*) Yes, do you like it?

Letty Oh, I *do*. It's *most* becoming. Has Arthur seen it?

Edith Not yet.

Letty Incidentally, he was so pleased and so *touched*, I think, when you suggested that as he was busy just now, you and I should receive this young man.

Edith I've never felt this was a matter for Arthur to deal with, Letty. I know exactly what his reaction would be. The moment he learnt of Anna's condition, he'd pack her off back to the village and wash his hands of the whole affair.

Letty Oh, I don't think so, Edith.

Edith But he's practically said as much, hasn't he?

Letty Arthur sometimes *says* things like that, but he doesn't really mean them, you know. By the way, he didn't show me the young man's letter, but I gather there was nothing in it to indicate the *real* reason for this visit, was there?

Edith Fortunately, no. It simply said that with Anna away in the country, here was a convenient opportunity to discuss her future well-being. That was the phrase he used.

Letty It really is a most peculiar situation, isn't it?

Edith How do you mean?

Letty Well, I mean here we are, about to confront a young man, a complete stranger, who's quite unaware that we already know what his relations with Anna must have been, and who, in any case, is expecting to meet Arthur.

Edith I see no problem there, Letty.

Letty What I mean is—to talk to Arthur, another man, is one thing, but faced by us he may well decide to avoid the issue completely.

Edith In that case, we shall be obliged at some stage to tell him exactly what we know and ask him point-blank what he proposes to do about it.

Letty I suppose so. Oh dear! But how embarrassing it could be. One can only hope he already has something in mind. Perhaps he'll put down a lump sum and set up a trust for the child. That's often done, I believe. ·

Edith Yes—well, in any event, he's obliged by law to make some provision for the child until it reaches a certain age. And if he doesn't do that, then he can be brought before the court to answer.

Letty But I imagine the sum of money the law would insist on is really quite small.

Edith It's totally inadequate. A few shillings a week.

Letty You seem to know a great deal about the subject, Edith.

Edith I should do. I spent a whole hour in the public library reading it up.

Letty Oh, I see. Well, in that case, I think I'd better leave most of the talking to you.

Edith I was just thinking, Letty . . .

Letty Yes?

Edith There's really no reason for both of us to confront Mr Bradford, is there?

Letty What!

Edith I was just wondering if it wouldn't be kinder, and perhaps a little less humiliating for him, if he had only one of us to deal with.

Letty Oh, no, Edith—that's not fair at all. It's essential that you should be present.

Unseen by Letty, Edith turns away, dismayed at being misunderstood

I should feel most uncomfortable, left on my own. I'm sure it'll be embarrassing enough as it is. No, no, you can't get out of it now, Edith

It's far too late for that.

Edith I'm not trying to get out of anything, Letty. In fact, if you're going to be so uncomfortable all the time, I should be quite happy to deal with Mr Bradford myself.

Letty You mean—see him alone?

Edith If it will make things easier for us all, why not?

Letty A tête-à-tête in these particular circumstances, Edith would seem to me to be highly improper.

Edith Surely the question is, simply, how can Anna's interests best be served, isn't it?

Letty Nevertheless, I'm quite certain Arthur would never have agreed . . .

Edith This has nothing whatever to do with Arthur . . .

Letty And I'd have thought the presence of a third party and an older person at that would have . . .

Suddenly a bell jangles towards the rear of the house

Oh, dear! Do you think . . . ?

Edith Yes. Come along, Letty—quickly!

Letty But I know Arthur expects me to be present, Edith, so I'm afraid I shall just have to insist.

Edith But don't you feel in this situation that one head would be better than two?

Letty No, I don't. I'm sorry, but I can't agree.

Edith (*grabbing Letty*) Oh, come along, Letty. (*She drags her towards the dining-room*)

Letty Oh, very well, Edith. It seems to me that sometimes you're not as simple as I thought you were.

Edith and Letty exit. The sound of their voices is cut off as the door closes. After a moment Sarah passes along the hall to the front door. There is a brief exchange of voices

Charles (*off*) My name's Bradford—I have an appointment with Mr Harnham.

Sarah (*off*) Yes, sir. Will you come this way.

Sarah admits the visitor and takes his hat. She then enters followed by Charles

Sarah If you'll just wait here, sir.

Charles Thank you.

Sarah exits

Charles looks about the room with interest. He is a well-built young man of pleasing appearance. He moves to examine one of the silver trophies, pausing to read the inscription on its base. Then, moving to the windows, he stands gazing out across the market square

Edith enters

Edith Good afternoon.
Charles (*swinging round*) Oh—Mrs Harnham?
Edith Yes.
Charles My name's Bradford—Charles Bradford.
Edith How do you do, Mr Bradford. We did meet, I think, just for a moment, didn't we—when the fair was here last?
Charles (*flattered*) Ah—so you remember?
Edith Perhaps because Anna has mentioned your name once or twice since. Do sit down.
Charles Thank you. (*He moves to a chair*) I'm sorry if I seem a nuisance, but I did write to Mr Harnham, as I expect you know . . .
Edith Of course. Unfortunately, just now my husband's entirely taken up with his business affairs, Mr Bradford, and it so happens, you see, that I've known Anna's family for donkey's years, and Anna in particular since she was quite tiny. So my husband felt that perhaps I could be of more help to you than he could. (*She sits*)
Charles I see. (*He sits*) Of course, I know from what Anna's told me how kind you've been, not only to her, but to the whole family.
Edith I've tried to do what little I could. The Dunsfords were a part of the village and very well-respected. Farmers, of course, and had been for generations. But when the bad times came in the late seventies, like so many others, they lost practically everything.
Charles And you made Anna your—your protégée, so to speak?
Edith When the parents died, there was an old aunt—and there was me. So I continued to take an interest in Anna, yes. And eventually I was able to find a place for her here.
Charles As a servant?
Edith As a servant, Mr Bradford. Of course, I still look on her as a mere child, although every now and then I realize, with something of a shock, that she's really quite grown-up.
Charles Oh, indeed—yes.

Sarah enters with a silver tray of tea things.

She's quite grown-up . . .
Edith In certain respects, at all events.

Sarah places the tray on a stool in front of Edith

(*Making polite conversation*) Do you know Salisbury at all well, Mr Bradford?
Charles Not really well, I'm afraid, although I've made several visits here recently, that is before I—er . . .
Edith Before the day of the fair, I expect you mean.
Charles Exactly.

Edith The cathedral is very fine, isn't it? (*As Sarah still hovers*) That'll do, Sarah.

Sarah goes out

They say it has the tallest spire in the whole of England.

Charles And I'm perfectly happy to agree with them, Mrs Harnham. (*Rising*) May we return to Anna?

Edith By all means.

Charles It would seem, so far as she's concerned, that you're acting *in loco parentis*. Isn't that so?

Edith Well, in the sense that, to a certain extent, I have made her interests my own—yes—but, of course, I've no legal standing whatsoever.

Charles No, no, but for all practical purposes such is the case. And that is why I'm here.

Edith Where is all this leading us, Mr Bradford?

Charles I'll come to that in a moment, Mrs Harnham. But first, I think I should tell you something about myself. May I?

Edith Yes, please do.

Charles I am, by profession, a barrister.

Edith (*surprised*) A barrister?

Charles Yes. At the moment I'm just a junior in chambers, barely existing on the few crumbs that fall from the high table. However, this is only a beginning. It won't always be so, I can assure you. It's not for me to say whether I'm brilliant or not, but I work hard, and on my feet I've a certain fluency which has already earned me several useful commendations. So I'm not without prospects. In short, I mean to get on, as they say.

Edith Sugar, Mr Bradford? How many?

Charles (*thrown*) Oh—two lumps, if you please.

Edith But why are you telling me all this? And what has it to do with Anna?

Charles I'm coming to that now, Mrs Harnham. You see, when I first saw her that evening at the fair, I'd not the slightest intention of ever becoming—oh, thank you.

Charles accepts a cup of tea from Edith but still stands

No—I went there simply to while away an hour or so, but having spent a miserable and lonely day, you'll understand it wasn't difficult to fall into conversation with Anna.

Edith Anna is a very natural girl, Mr Bradford.

Charles (*eagerly*) Yes, isn't she?

Edith Some would perhaps call her—ingenuous.

Charles If you mean there's a certain innocence about her, I agree. That's what I found so engaging. Then, as you probably know, we had a further meeting, Anna and I.

Edith The day after the fair?

Charles Yes—let me tell you what happened . . .

Edith (*hurriedly*) You're letting your tea get cold, Mr Bradford.

Charles gulps some of his tea, puts down his cup, then resumes

Charles Well, we spent a delightful afternoon together. But such encounters in this enlightened age are not altogether uncommon, and normally, in a day or two, I'd have forgotten the whole incident. (*Pause*) But I didn't.

Edith No?

Charles Oh, I can understand very well that to you Anna must seem just another little girl from the village, with all the limitations that implies. But you see, I've had the good fortune to discover qualities in Anna which I'm sure you're quite unaware of.

Edith How can you have done? You were only . . .

Charles I know what you're going to say. I was only here for two days. But since then, Mrs Harnham, Anna and I have been writing to each other.

Edith (*after a pause*) Really?

Charles Yes—twice a week at least—sometimes more often than that. If you'll allow me to . . . (*From an inside pocket of his jacket he produces a fat bundle of letters tied with tape*) There! And I'm not ashamed to admit that I know several of them by heart.

Edith Your correspondent would be highly flattered to hear that.

Charles It's perfectly true. I could recite one now, if you wish.

Edith Oh, no, please! It's just that I'm a little surprised to learn that Anna has the ability to express herself so effectively.

Charles Quite frankly, so was I. But that's what I find so delightful. Her sentiments, you see, are so fresh, so obviously those of a young girl of such—well—such tenderness and generosity that only a fellow with a heart of stone could fail to respond.

Edith You make her sound a paragon, Mr Bradford.

Charles Ah, I see what it is. You think I'm overstating the case, don't you?

Edith Well, I'm not really in a position to judge that, am I?

Charles Then in one moment you will be, Mrs Harnham. (*He slips out the top envelope from the bundle*) I'd like, if I may, to show you just one letter.

Edith (*protesting*) Oh, but surely . . .

Charles Absolutely in confidence, of course . . . It's one of the early ones. It won't embarrass you in any way, I can promise. But it will give you an idea. There . . .

He unfolds the chosen letter, hands it to Edith. Edith glances at the letter merely to identify it, then puts a hand over her eyes in a gesture compounded of embarrassment and desperation

Well?

Edith It's certainly literate. I think I can say that much.

Charles Oh, come now. You can say much more than that, Mrs Harnham.

Don't you agree she writes very prettily?

Edith Well, if she's pleased you—then, there's your answer, isn't it? (*She hands back the letter*)

Charles Mrs Harnham—let me come to the point. For weeks past now, Anna's hardly been out of my thoughts for a moment, so you'll understand that what I'm going to say is carefully considered and comes only after much heart-searching.

Edith Well, of course.

Charles I won't pretend there haven't been times when I had doubts, but not any longer. Those doubts were finally swept away by one particular letter which I have here. It's quite recent.

Edith Oh?

Charles It concerns a private matter which I won't bother *you* with, Mrs Harnham, except to say that, whereas the attitude of most young girls in similar circumstances would have been one of complete self-interest this is not so with Anna. Instead, in this particular letter Anna shows an unselfishness, indeed a nobility of character which I, for one, never dreamt of finding in *any* woman.

Edith (*nervously*) Oh, come, Mr Bradford! You obviously haven't looked very far, have you?

Charles It was this letter which decided me to come down here and make my intentions clear to those most concerned with Anna's welfare, because—tomorrow I mean to ask her to marry me.

Edith Marry you, Mr Bradford?

Charles Yes—as soon as can conveniently be arranged.

Edith rises slowly

You don't approve?

Edith, agitated, moves away to the windows

Edith Oh, no! I didn't say *that*. I should be delighted, of course, for Anna to make a suitable match. Her future happiness is very much my concern. (*Turning*) On the other hand . . .

Charles On the other hand?

Edith Anna is what she is—a simple girl with little or no knowledge of the world at large, while you, I now learn, are a professional man with your whole career in front of you.

Charles (*cheerfully*) Mrs Harnham, if I thought it was necessary, for the sake of Anna, I'd give up my profession tomorrow.

Edith (*appalled*) Oh, no!

Charles (*laughing*) Oh, please don't be alarmed. I see no necessity to do any such thing. But I think I know what's disturbing you.

Edith (*flustered*) Do you, Mr Bradford? (*She puts her hand on the desk drawer where she keeps Charles's letters*)

Charles Yes—you're afraid that I might be asking too much of her.

Edith And aren't you?

Charles I don't think so.

Edith But as you rise in your profession, Mr Bradford, do you think Anna will be able to fulfil all the requirements of her position as your wife?

Charles I can't see why not. With her powers of development and perhaps after a little coaching in the social forms of life in London, she'll make as good a professional man's wife as anyone could hope for.

Edith Yes, but then there's your family. You have your family to consider, surely? What do they think?

Charles Apart from an unmarried sister a lot older than I am, I've no close ties now.

Edith But the fact remains, the pair of you are barely acquainted, you've seen so little of each other . . .

Charles For the very good reason that I've had to keep my nose to the grindstone, but if the knowledge one has of another person is essentially a matter of communication, which it undoubtedly is——

Edith sits at her desk. With seeming casualness she pulls open the drawer and looks down at the letters from Charles which lie there. She is almost at the point of confession

—then there can be no two people who know each other better than Anna and I do at this moment. Aren't I right?

Edith Oh, yes. I know very well just how much letters can mean to one— but—but surely they can never take the place of the actual—the loved one?

Charles No—but sometimes, I think, it's good for us to have to put our thoughts into words, Mrs Harnham. We learn things about ourselves we'd never have believed. I know I have. And I'm sure Anna has, too.

Edith Has she?

Charles It's not easy, perhaps, for us to put ourselves in her place—a girl of her age. Perhaps we've forgotten how exciting it all was. That growing wonder of waking up into a new world for the first time and realizing that until now one has only been half alive. I find it all here in her letters to me.

Edith (*shaken*) Do you?

Charles Oh, yes—quite clearly.

Edith closes the drawer then, to recover her composure, moves back to the sofa

Edith Will you have some more tea, Mr Bradford?

Charles No, thank you. Then—may I take it you're not wholly against the plan, Mrs Harnham?

Edith (*sitting*) I'm not wholly against it—no—it's just that I—I've hardly had time to consider it. But any decision, of course, must be Anna's.

Charles Of course. Judging by the letters, I fancy *her* mind is already made up. Now, if I may trespass a little further on your kindness and ask for your co-operation.

Edith Co-operation?

Charles Yes. (*He produces a small pocket-diary and sits close beside her*) (*Briskly*) Now I thought a suitable day for the wedding would be the fifth of August, which this year falls on a Saturday. That allows us four weeks precisely in which to make our arrangements. But would that be a convenient day for you?

Edith Do you mean you wish her to be married from here—from this house?

Charles If you agree. It's sensible, isn't it?

Edith (*weakly*) I don't know whether my husband . . . ?

Charles It'll only be a civil ceremony, of course.

Edith Oh—not in church?

Charles I know Anna's circumstances, Mrs Harnham—her financial circumstances, I mean—and I know my own. We're going to need every penny we can scrape together. The registrar's office is not far from here, I imagine?

Edith It's just across the square.

Charles Good. I shall stay overnight at *The White Horse*. I dare say Anna would like to have some few friends or relatives of her own present at the ceremony—what do you think?

Edith There'll have to be witnesses, of course. And then, Mr Bradford?

Charles (*with self-mockery*) And then, Mrs Harnham? Why, then we shall catch the train back to London and there live happily ever after.

Edith I see. And do you intend to set up house in London?

Charles Ah! I'm afraid funds won't run to that—not immediately, that is. But I have my eye on some very comfortable rooms in Bloomsbury.

Edith I'm afraid I don't know London at all.

Charles No? Well, Bloomsbury's just between the West End and the City. I'm sure Anna will be delighted with Bloomsbury.

Edith (*with feeling*) Anna will be in paradise, Mr Bradford.

Charles (*pleased*) You think so? I'm so glad you think so. Of course, I know a lot of people would say that to start married life with no money in the bank is sheer madness. But when one's in love one's already a little mad, don't you think?

Edith Oh, yes.

Charles In a rather exciting way. And to have someone who'll gladly put up with the lean years is to build two lives on a firmer foundation than mere pounds, shillings and pence. Then, after a year or two, when one's a success and comes to look back, surely it's to find that the early worries and disappointments have only served to strengthen the love each has for the other.

Edith (*slowly*) Yes—that—that is how marriage should be.

There is a pause. Charles rises, then Edith

Charles Well, I must thank you, Mrs Harnham, for letting me take up so much of your time.

Edith You return to London tomorrow, Mr Bradford? (*She goes and pulls the bell-rope*)

Charles Late tomorrow. Naturally, I'm hoping to see something of Anna before I go.

Edith Naturally. And she's expecting to see you. Mansell will be bringing her back this evening.

Charles Then thank you again, Mrs Harnham. Oh—one small thing. You won't—I mean—I know you'll understand, but I'd like to be the one to *tell* Anna.

Edith Of course. And I hope you'll be down here again soon, now that—now that you've made up your mind.

Charles I'd like very much to think so, but I doubt if it'll be possible before the wedding.

Edith Oh, dear! Why ever not?

Charles (*with a wry laugh*) Mainly because I'm obliged to keep on good terms with my clerk in chambers.

Edith How on earth does your clerk come into it?

Charles He fixes me up with work, you see—usually out of Town and on Fridays—briefs that nobody else can be bothered with. But if you're never seen, you'll never get known; so, with an eye to the future, I take what comes and as solicitors are already beginning to ask for me by name, I feel I'm heading in the right direction.

Edith Then you'll see nothing of Anna?

Charles I'm afraid not. We shall just have to continue our courtship by correspondence.

Sarah appears in the hallway and picks up Charles's hat

Edith (*worried*) Yes, I—I suppose you will.

Charles Good-bye, Mrs Harnham—and thank you.

Edith Good-bye, Mr Bradford.

Charles goes out and off towards the front door, followed by Sarah

For a moment, Edith remains quite still then, as she hears the sound of the door opening, she hurries to the window, pressing close to the glass to catch a last glimpse of the departing Charles

So engrossed is Edith that when Sarah returns for the tea-tray, she fails to notice her. Sarah gives her mistress a curious look and goes off. Letty enters from the dining-room

Letty Well?

Edith (*turning from the window*) Oh, I was just . . .

Letty What happened, Edith? Did you come to a satisfactory arrangement?

Edith A satisfactory arrangement? Yes, Letty, I suppose one could call it that.

Letty Oh? He's agreed to make reasonable provision for the child?

Edith (*flatly*) He's going to marry her.

Letty Marry her? Well! Good gracious! You do surprise me, Edith. *Marry* her. I never expected to hear that. Of course, it's perfectly right that he should, but it so seldom turns out that way, especially when there are such differences of background. I wonder *why* he decided to marry her?

Edith Because he thinks he's in love with her.

Letty And isn't he?

Edith No.

Letty How can you be so certain?

Edith I know Anna.

Letty I don't understand.

Edith He's in love with the person he *imagines* her to be.

Letty Edith dear, don't be so fanciful. Nothing imaginary about the girl's condition, is there?

Edith (*moving to the desk*) If it's not to prove a disaster, Anna must be turned into something nearer that young man's idea of her.

Letty But surely the ceremony will have to be quite soon—in the circumstances, won't it?

Edith Yes, the wedding is to take place exactly four weeks today.

Letty Four weeks! Do you seriously imagine that Anna can be transformed quite so rapidly?

Edith She must be, Letty, oh she must be . . .

Edith sits at her desk as—

the CURTAIN *falls*

SCENE 2

The same. A Tuesday morning, three days later.
Anna, in cap and apron over her print dress, sits at the desk, pen in hand, labouring over her copy-book. Sarah, similarly dressed, moves quickly about the room returning recently cleaned silver pieces to their various positions, from a tray on the sofa table

Sarah Bertie was making such a fuss—so I said why don't you ask if you can speak to Mr Philips, the manager at the maltings? But Bertie's ever so shy that way. He never wants to step out of line or nothing. Only I kept on nagging at him and it was a lucky thing I did.

Anna (*not looking up*) So?

Sarah Well, he did get to see him in the end. And Mr Philips says there's bound to be a house come up *if* this business with Tremlett's goes all right. I mean Bertie's done over twelve years at Harnham's and he's right up the list, so now we just got to keep our fingers crossed.

Anna (*turning on her chair to face the room*) But how lovely though, Sarah, when you *do* get a house.

Sarah Walking out's all right in the summer time, but in the winter where can you go to? You can't. You've been lucky—being so quick. You don't hardly know you're born, you don't.

Anna Yes, I do, Sarah. My Charles isn't rich or anything like that. We'll have to go ever so carefully—to start with anyway.

Sarah Still, he isn't exactly what I'd call poor though, is he?

Anna Well, *we're* not having a house—only furnished rooms.

Sarah Never mind that, you'll be living like a lady, won't you? So what will you do all day?

Anna One thing, I shan't be lonely. Charles has ever such a lot of nice friends, and, in time, I shall get to know all of them. Charles says, if I like, I can have an afternoon tea-party every day until I do.

Sarah Every *day*?

Anna Well—perhaps not *every* day. I expect some days I shall be out paying calls myself.

Sarah (*impressed*) Paying calls, eh? My! Aren't you cool!

Anna But that's what life's like in London, Sarah. Everybody pays calls. Charles did try to explain it to me. Some things are done, he says, and some things are not done. So I should think to begin with, I shall be quite busy finding out which is which.

Sarah I should say! But suppose you go and make a mistake?

Anna Then what happens is next time you walk down the street all the people look the other way and nobody says good morning.

Sarah Ooh! The stuck-up lot! I wouldn't like that sort of going on.

Anna No—only with my Charles there beside me telling me what's what, I shan't feel too bad. (*Turning back to the desk*) Here, look out, Sarah— she'll be down in a moment and I'm meant to have this whole page done by then.

Sarah (*approaching Anna*) Let's have a look.

Anna No, go on—it's private.

Sarah No, it's not. That's only your old copy-book, that's all that is.

Anna (*covering up*) All the same, it's private, if you don't mind.

Sarah Oh, come on—let's have a look.

Anna It's not even interesting—truly. It's nothing really—only words.

Sarah Then what's it matter? Let's see.

Anna You won't be no wiser if I let you. Oh, all right then—there.

Sarah (*peering over Anna's shoulder*) What's it say? (*Reading*) "Charles Bradford. Charles Bradford. Charles Bradford." That first line there's not your writing, Anna—that's madam's.

Anna Because it's the copy, stupid.

Sarah (*reading*) "Belov'd. Belov'd. Belov'd." And that's her writing, too.

Anna I *told* you! She writes it out, then I copy them out over and over.

Sarah Why? Are you trying to get to write just like madam does?

Anna That's what she wants, but I'll never be able to, not if I was to sit here till kingdom come.

Sarah (*head on one side*) I see what it is. *She* writes pointed. Yours is more round. I like the way she does her big B's though. She does her big B's lovely, only that's a funny word—belov'd.

Anna Bel*oved*. It's what I call him in the letters.

Sarah Oh? I see. It's still funny though, isn't it?

Anna I never really liked it much myself, but she thought it was nice, so . . .

Sarah Madam did? Then what's he call you—if I'm not being too nosey?

Anna He calls me dearest.

Sarah Dearest. Is that *all*?

Anna Well—in the letters. He's different, of course, when . . . What's Bertie call you?

Sarah Bertie? Now what does he call me? Oh, all sorts really. Sometimes he'll call me love. "Hello, me old love," he'll say. Or sometimes he'll just call me Sal, like "Well, how's me old Sal today?" That's his style. Oh, he's quite a card.

Arthur emerges from the study. He is about to leave for the brewery and carries a sheaf of documents

Arthur Ah! Mrs Harnham about anywhere?

Anna She's upstairs, sir, in the sewing-room.   ⎫ *Speaking*

Sarah She's upstairs, marking the new linen, sir. ⎭ *together*

Arthur (*to Sarah*) Then slip up and tell her I'm just off, would you, Sarah.

Sarah Yes, sir.

Sarah goes out and up the stairs

Arthur (*sitting on the sofa*) Well, Anna? So Mrs Harnham tells me you'll soon be leaving us.

Anna Yes, sir. Three weeks on Saturday, sir.

Arthur (*checking through his papers*) Wedding-bells, eh? I'm delighted to hear it.

Anna Thank you, sir.

Arthur And you've made a pretty good catch, I understand.

Anna I hope so, sir.

Arthur Hope so? No good living in hopes, you know. You need to be damned sure.

Anna Yes, sir. I am, sir.

Arthur Good. Now I don't know what your arrangements are, Anna, but when our girls leave to get married, what usually happens is, after the ceremony, we have the friends and relations back here, to drink a toast to the happy couple and that sort of thing.

Anna Oh, I think that would be lovely, sir.

Arthur Then I'll have a word with Mrs Harnham. We let Cook take over the breakfast-room and I must say she usually does it rather welll.

Anna How kind of you, sir. Thank you, sir.

Arthur Come to think of it, you've both got a lot to thank me for—the pair of you.

Anna Have we, sir?

Arthur It *is* the young feller you met at the fair, isn't it?

Anna Oh, yes, sir.

Arthur Well then? Don't you remember crying your eyes out because madam wasn't going to let you follow it up? Why, if I hadn't come

along when I did, you might never have seen him again.
Anna I know, sir. Thank you, sir.

Sarah starts down the stairs

Arthur Anyhow, it all ended happily, that's the main thing. But that doesn't always happen, you know.
Sarah (*from the hallway*) Madam's just coming, sir.
Arthur Thank you, Sarah.

Sarah goes off towards the rear of the house

(*With a nod at the desk*) What are you supposed to be doing now? Writing?
Anna Yes, sir. Madam's set me a whole page of writing to do.
Arthur I'd have thought you got enough practice writing letters to your young man.
Anna Oh, I don't write those, sir.
Arthur Oh?
Anna No, sir. Madam writes those, sir.
Arthur Madam does?

Edith comes downstairs

Anna Yes, sir.
Arthur Does she. I *see*.

Edith enters the room

Anna sits at the desk and writes as fast as she can

Edith Yes, Arthur.
Arthur Oh, there you are, Edith. I was just telling Anna that after the wedding, if she likes, she can bring her friends and relations back here.
Edith Oh? But . . .
Arthur It's something we've always done—not perhaps in your time, but we've always done it—given our girls something of a send-off.
Edith But there'll be no occasion for that, Arthur. There'll barely be time for them to catch the London train as it is.
Arthur Then let them catch a later train.
Edith I don't think that, under the circumstances . . .
Arthur You ask Letty. She'll tell you. (*Laughing*) I remember once we put up a barrel of our special home brew for them, and the next morning—the next morning—Letty found one old man still fast asleep under the sideboard.
Edith (*not amused*) Really?
Arthur You ask her. Anyhow, we'll see. Plenty of time to talk about that later.

Edith Yes. Have you finished, Anna?

Anna No, not quite, ma'am.

Edith You should be by now. What on earth have you been doing?

Arthur Yes—well, I'm just off, Edith. All I wanted to say was that I'm lunching with Tremlett before the meeting and it's likely to be a long one. We're giving him a seat on the board, of course, but it's the end of the road so far as he's concerned. And yet he can't see it, you know—can't see it. Poor fellow. (*He laughs*)

Arthur goes into the hall, picks up his hat and goes off towards the front door

Edith Let me see what you've done.

Anna hands the copy-book to Edith who studies it for a moment

Anna, this is *not* good enough. It really isn't. I can't believe you're even trying.

Anna I am, ma'am, truly I am. It's just that I can't do it like you, ma'am.

Edith But with the copy staring you in the face surely it's not too much to ask you to *spell* the words correctly. Look—you've left the *e* out of Charles all the way down the page.

Anna Have I, ma'am?

Edith Yes, you have.

Anna I didn't mean to, ma'am.

Edith It's just carelessness. The fact is you're not putting your mind to it. (*Desperately*) And you must, Anna, you must! I'd have thought, for the sake of someone you say you love, you'd have been only too anxious to work hard at your writing. If you're not prepared to make even this small sacrifice, then what kind of a wife are you going to be, Anna?

Anna (*rather sullenly*) Once we're married, what'll it all matter?

Edith That may well be something you've yet to discover. But you're *not* married, Anna—not yet. There are nearly four more weeks until the wedding-day, and that means at least seven or eight *more* letters have still to be written. *Who* is going to write *them*?

Anna Well—you'll have to, ma'am, I suppose.

Edith Oh, if only you'd made more progress, Anna. Even if I'd had to help you with the sentiments, at least you could have written the letters yourself. As it is—(*she drops the copy-book on to the desk*)—there's only one thing I can do.

Anna How do you mean, ma'am?

Edith He must be told, of course. He must be told everything.

Anna (*alarmed*) No, ma'am.

Edith (*firmly*) He must be told that all this time, I've been answering his letters for you.

Anna But why, ma'am? Why do you have to tell him now?

Edith Because, once you're married, he's bound to find out—sooner or later. Then think of all the miserable recriminations that would begin . . .

Anna But if you tell him now, ma'am, he might change his mind and not marry me at all.

Edith That should be for him to decide, Anna. And the poor fellow must be given the opportunity to do so in the full knowledge of all the circumstances.

Anna (*distressed*) Oh, ma'am! But what would I *do*? What would *happen* to me? I think if he was to change his mind now I'd—I'd make an end to myself.

Edith Anna! Don't ever say such a wicked thing!

Anna I would, ma'am. For what kind of a life should I look forward to?

Edith But can't you see that a marriage built on a deceit—on a mere trick, if you like—because that's how it'll seem to him—could so easily become the most bitter and loveless existence imaginable?

Anna But once we're married, I shan't need to worry about the old letters because I know, from going with him, I can make him happy. I know that. And at those times, ma'am, he's never bothering himself about grammar or spellin' or fine words or any things like that.

Edith (*stung*) There are other times to consider, Anna. And let me tell you this: it was the *letters* and *only* the letters that made him decide to marry you.

Anna No! No, it wasn't, ma'am, it wasn't.

Edith *My* letters, Anna.

Anna But it's me he wants—not old letters. Over and over, he's told me that. It's *me*.

Edith Oh yes, in a physical sense, I'm sure he finds you wholly desirable. I don't doubt that for a moment. But to give his sudden passion some lasting value, he was looking for something more. Well, he found it— in my letters.

Anna You *say* that.

Edith He told me.

Anna is deeply upset

Edith So now you see, don't you, how terribly wicked it would be not to tell him the truth?

A sullen silence from Anna

You do see, don't you?

Anna (*stoutly*) No, I *don't* see. How can letters matter, whatever you put, set beside what the two of us have been to each other?

Edith If you'd shown more concern for what was written in the letters instead of leaving it all to me, you'd not ask such a foolish question.

Anna I tried—I did try to at the start, only in the end they were always written your way.

Edith Yes, but *his* letters? Why, apart from wanting to know when he was coming again, you've never shown the slightest interest in his letters, either.

Anna It's just that I've grown to feel they're not much to do with me.

Edith No. And in a sense, they're not. But Mr Bradford doesn't feel that. Each letter from him has marked a step forward to which I always had to respond. So it's not you he's come to know, Anna, but me.

Anna Only in his head. But me—he knows me. He *really* knows me. He's never even touched you.

Edith I don't care, Anna. I cannot go on. I shouldn't go on. And it's not only him I'm thinking of—I'm thinking of the effect it's having on me.

Anna On you, ma'am?

Edith Yes.

Anna But it can't have any effect on *you*, ma'am.

Edith How can you say that?

Anna Because . . .

Edith Well?

Anna Because you're married already.

Edith Oh, you poor, stupid little fool! Can't you see what it's meant to me to have had to write to this man for weeks on end? And to write in terms which are now virtually those of a wife? Can't you see? To have had to lay bare my deepest, most intimate feelings and then—oh, God! —pretend—pretend to a physical condition which, in fact, isn't mine at all? Can you imagine what that's meant to me and still say it can't have had any effect on me?

Anna But, ma'am . . .

Edith Every letter from him, I read as if it were meant for me. Every letter I wrote was written from *my* heart and nobody else's. And I won him, Anna. *I* won him.

Anna (*desperately*) You didn't! You didn't!

Edith (*almost shouting in Anna's ear*) Do you think a man like him would have let himself be captured by a common, ignorant servant girl?

Anna flinches and hides her face

Those were *my* thoughts and *my* feelings he responded to, and for the first time in my life I feel I'm no longer alone. I've someone to love and care about—even though to him I'm hardly so much as a name. But it cannot go on—it cannot go on.

Edith, overcome, sinks down and sobs. For a moment Anna struggles mentally with the dimly perceived implications of Edith's words, then she moves quickly to her mistress and kneels beside her

Anna I haven't rightly understood. But now I see—of course. (*Pause*) You love him too, don't you?

Edith lifts her face to Anna, a movement which Anna rightly interprets to be an affirmation

Oh, ma'am!

The two women remain silent for a moment, pressed close, grasping each other, seeking comfort

Edith Forgive me, Anna. Forgive me.

Anna Don't be upset so, ma'am. You've been so good and kind to me——

Edith But I haven't, I haven't.

Anna —there's nothing to forgive.

Edith I've been selfish and foolish. I am to blame for everything—everything.

Anna No, ma'am, no.

Edith Yes—I should have seen what was happening, but I wouldn't. And I wouldn't because—I *wanted* to go on. And—oh, I still do.

Anna (*after a pause*) It only started because I asked you to help me. You were only trying to do what was best for me.

Edith Of course. For who else *could* have helped you, Anna? You had nobody. At the start, you were my only concern.

Anna Am I not still, ma'am?

Edith Yes, yes, of course you are, but . . .

Anna Then I know you'll not forsake me now, ma'am.

Edith But now we have to think of him too, Anna.

Anna I do think of him—all the time, ma'am.

Edith Then surely you'd never wish to deceive him?

Anna But, ma'am, I'm not. Truly I'm not. For whatever nice things you put in the letters, you could never have put anything nicer than what I'm thinking every blessed minute of the day, and when it comes to thinking of him I do have a niceness of my own.

Edith Of course you have, Anna.

Anna And I'm sure, if I'd been able, what I'd have put down for myself would have meant the same as what you put, ma'am.

Edith If you'd been *able*—that's the very point, Anna. As it is, he believes you to have an ability which you simply don't possess.

Anna And because I don't, is that why you think I'm not good enough for him?

Edith I shouldn't have said that, Anna. I was upset. But that's what the world will think.

Anna Then—that's what he's going to think, too.

Edith He may not.

Anna Ma'am—if you was to write and tell him everything—now—this very minute—do you truly believe, right deep down, that he'd ever marry me?

Edith How can either of us know what he'd do, Anna? On the one hand, I have his letters—on the other hand, you . . .

Anna I have his baby, ma'am.

There is the sound of footsteps. Anna gets to her feet and moves quickly away from Edith

Sarah comes down the hallway and goes up the stairs

Oh, please don't tell him, ma'am. If we was to go on as we did for just a little longer, it can't make so much difference to you, but—oh, ma'am, the difference to me!

Edith remains impassive. Anna tries again

If I should marry him I'll be as good as gold to him. I swear I will, and put myself out to learn all the things I need to know.

Pause

Perhaps he won't find out about the letters, not to start off with. Why should he? Perhaps by then, ma'am, I'll have had the baby. He's not the sort to turn against his own, is he? Not him.

Pause

So why shouldn't he be happy, ma'am, up there in London with me?

Pause

And if he *is* happy, ma'am, then that's what we both want, isn't it?

Edith (*speaking from a preoccupation of her own*) Do you realize that you'll be asked to sign your name by the registrar, Anna? (*Rising*) So you'd better concentrate your attention on learning to write it the way I do.

Anna (*slowly*) You mean—you—you'll go on with writing the letters, ma'am?

Edith I shall hate myself, but I shall go on.

Anna Oh, ma'am! Thank you, ma'am, for now I'm sure everything'll come right because you always know what's best to do.

Anna seizes Edith's hand and kisses it

Edith Oh, Anna! If one knew that . . .

Both remain motionless as the Lights fade, and—

the CURTAIN *falls*

SCENE 3

The same. The morning of the wedding

Letty enters with a jug of water, goes to the sofa table and starts unwrapping some roses which have just arrived from the florist. Arthur, in high spirits, emerges from the study carrying a copy of "The Times"

Arthur I say, Letty, look at this. We're in *The Times*. Quite a decent bit. (*He hands Letty the paper, folded in such a way that she can read the column heading*)

Letty Why, so we are! (*Reading*) "Harnham's gains control of Tremlett's. Further extension of brewing interests in the South West."

Arthur Go on.

Letty (*reading*) "The chairman of Harnham's, Mr Arthur Harnham, told our representative, 'This will make Harnham's not only the oldest but by far the largest firm of brewers in the South-West of England.'"

Arthur Not bad, is it? The whole of the South-West. (*Seeing the roses*)

Hello? Where've those come from?

Letty Anna's young man—the bridegroom.

Arthur Oh? Who are they for?

Letty (*starting to arrange the roses in bowls*) They were addressed to all of us, but I suspect they're really meant for Edith.

Arthur I see. Yes, I'd be the happiest man in England today if . . . (*He moves to the windows*) I suppose they'll be back any moment now, won't they?

Letty Yes, it doesn't take many minutes in a registry office.

Arthur (*gazing out at the square*) No.

Letty You've seen the masterpiece Cook's brought forth, I suppose?

Arthur (*his thoughts elsewhere*) Yes, I have—yes. How they love that sort of thing, don't they? (*There is a pause, then he suddenly turns to Letty*) I don't blame the girl, of course I don't, but I must admit I'm damn glad to see her go.

Letty Edith will be terribly upset. You'll have to be very gentle with her for a little while.

Arthur If I ever have the chance to get near her!

Letty You'll have more chance now, Arthur. It's going to be very much easier for you both.

Arthur How do you mean?

Letty I'm going away.

Arthur What?

Letty I'm leaving here, Arthur.

Arthur You don't mean that.

Letty Yes, I do. I'm going to live in Weymouth near Cousin Maisie.

Arthur But why?

Letty I shall be happier, I think. You see, you have Edith, and Edith doesn't need *me*, I assure you.

Arthur But who's going to look after everything? I mean . . .

Letty She will, of course. You'll find her just as competent as I ever was, Arthur.

Arthur But—does she know you're going?

Letty Not yet. It's been a very emotional time for Edith, so I thought I'd wait until the wedding was over.

Arthur I see. (*Pause*) She locks her bedroom door now. Did you know that?

Letty No, I—I'm sorry, Arthur.

Arthur Do you think it would do any good, once Anna's gone, if you were to talk to Edith?

Letty (*firmly*) No, Arthur.

Arthur She might tell *you* things that . . .

Letty Arthur, you once said I played the match-maker rather well. Perhaps I played it too well and for rather too long.

Arthur How do you mean?

Letty If I'd had any sense, I should have gone from here the day you got married.

Arthur Why?

Letty Because without me here to act as go between, you and Edith would have simply had to come to terms with each other.

Arthur (*testily*) Come to terms with each other? What's the good of that? We have come to terms—that's half the trouble. But a marriage is not just a question of coming to terms with somebody. Really, Letty—you sometimes . . .

Letty What I'm saying is, we all have to put up with each other's short-comings if we live under the same roof, and I think you'll both learn to do that more quickly if I'm not here.

Sarah bursts noisily in through the front door, wearing her best summer dress and hat, with a corsage of flowers

Sarah Oh, ma'am, he's such a lovely feller. You'd never believe. A real gentleman he is. But ever so nice and friendly with it—(*seeing Arthur*) —oh, beg pardon, sir.

Arthur So it's all over, is it? Man and wife now, eh?

Sarah Yes, sir.

Arthur Well, I'll be in the study. I must try to think of something suitable to say. They'll expect a few well chosen words no doubt.

Letty Of course they will, Arthur.

Arthur Yes. What you're proposing, Letty—and I don't say you're wrong, mind—but I can't see it's the answer. It'll change things—bound to— but I can't see the answer there.

Arthur goes off into the study

Sarah And look—look what he give us, ma'am. (*She indicates her spray of flowers*) He give 'em to all the ladies.

Letty How very pretty, Sarah.

Sarah And a white carnation each for the gentlemen—all done up in silver paper,

Letty Did everything go quite smoothly at the ceremony?

Sarah Oh, perfect, ma'am. Mind, it's not like in church, is it? You don't get none of that feeling come over you and it's so lovely you want to cry. You don't get none of that. But it was a dear little wedding all the same.

Letty They'll be here any minute, I suppose?

Sarah Madam wanted me back here to show the others where to go, so I rushed on over while they're having the photograph.

Letty Well, that shouldn't take long.

Sarah No—only I come straight across the square, ma'am, but I expect the others'll go the long way round.

Letty Why?

Sarah Because they're still putting up the stalls and the swings and that.

Letty I'd forgotten about the fair. Really—it seems no time at all since it was last here.

Sarah August bank holiday on Monday, ma'am. And the new steam roundabout, that's back here again. Do you think Cook and me will be able to slip out for a short while on Monday, ma'am?

Letty I dare say, but that's something you'll have to ask Mrs Harnham.

Sarah Cook's made ever such a lovely little wedding cake, ma'am, with a pink horseshoe right in the middle.

Letty I'm sure Anna will be delighted.

Sarah She was ever so nervous, ma'am. When it come for her to sign the form, her hand was shaking so she could hardly write.

Letty I expect you'll be just as nervous on your wedding-day, Sarah.

Sarah *My* wedding-day! I hope I live to see it, ma'am, the way things are.

Letty Nonsense! It'll be your turn next, I expect.

Sarah Mr Harnham hasn't said nothing more about a house for us, has he?

Letty He's been so busy lately. But now that this Tremlett affair is settled there'll be several houses falling vacant. I'll speak to him again.

Sarah Oh, thank you, ma'am. Only Bert says he thinks Mr Philips has forgotten all about it, too.

Noise and movement in the street outside catch Sarah's attention and she moves quickly to the windows

It's them, ma'am. They've come in a fly. Just the two of them. And he's helping her out.

Letty Then you go and show them in, Sarah.

Sarah Yes, ma'am. Well, won't it seem funny, ma'am—me calling Anna Dunsford "Mrs Charles Bradford".

Sarah goes into the hall as Anna and Charles enter from the front door

'Ere, you shouldn't have come in like that, you got to be properly announced. (*She enters the room*) Mr and Mrs Charles Bradford. (*She giggles*)

Anna Oh, Sarah!

Anna and Charles come into the room. Sarah remains by the hall

Letty Well, Anna? Come in, my dear, and tell me how it feels to be Mrs Charles Bradford.

Anna It feels very nice, ma'am. This is Charles, ma'am.

Letty Oh, how do you do, Mr Bradford? I'm Mrs Harnham's sister-in-law.

Charles How do you do?

Letty (*grasping his hand with both of hers*) May I wish you both every happiness for the future and many, many golden years together.

Charles Thank you—that's most kind of you. (*He glances at Anna*) I fancy we're both still feeling somewhat tongue-tied, perhaps even a little bewildered by our sudden change of status. Aren't we, Anna, my dear?

Anna Yes, Charles.

Charles But I'm told that is something we'll grow accustomed to quite soon enough.

Letty Is Mrs Harnham . . . ?

Anna She should be here any moment, ma'am.

Charles She insisted on walking, I may say, but only so that Anna and I would be alone together in the fly.

Anna As we drove round the square, we could see the workmen putting up the new steam roundabout, couldn't we, Charles?

Charles We saw the very horse Anna was riding that evening last May when we met for the first time.

Anna A white one with a long black mane.

Charles Unhappily, it was in a rather undignified position lying on its back with its legs in the air.

Everyone laughs

Letty How very unromantic of it!

Sarah (*from the hallway*) Here's madam now.

Edith appears in the hallway. Like Sarah, she wears a spray of flowers pinned to her dress. Briskly, she at once takes charge

Edith Is everything ready in the breakfast-room, Sarah?

Sarah Yes, ma'am.

Edith Then I think we should go along now. (*To Charles and Anna*) There's not a great deal of time before you two must set out for the station.

Charles (*looking at his pocket-watch*) Not to cut it too fine, Mrs Harnham, I've told the fellow on the fly that he's to wait for us.

Edith Yes, it's sometimes difficult to find one on a Saturday. Now come along, Anna—Sarah. Cook has a lovely surprise waiting for you.

As Anna and Sarah move off along the hall towards the breakfast-room, Anna is showing her wedding ring to Sarah. They go off

(*To Letty*) Does Arthur know we're back?

Letty Oh, he's bound to have heard, Edith. He's only in the study.

Edith Then come along, Mr Bradford.

Edith and Letty move into the hall, followed by Charles. As the two women move off towards the breakfast-room, the study door opens and Arthur appears in time to detain Charles

Arthur Ah, Bradford? I'm Harnham.

Charles How do you do, sir?

Arthur Everything went off all right, I hope?

Charles Oh, splendidly, sir.

Arthur Good. Then I think, before the revels start, my lad, we'd better just have a word together, you and I, eh?

Charles Certainly, sir.

Arthur grips Charles by the arm in a friendly manner and leads him back into the room

Arthur Don't be afraid. I'm not proposing to make a long speech or anything of that sort. I know you've a train to catch, but they're expecting a *few* words from me, of course. And you'll have to reply.

Charles I think I can manage that, sir.

Arthur But the thing is, in the ordinary way, these affairs are entirely local and everybody knows everybody else. But this is different. Down here, you're what we call a foreigner—a bit of a dark horse. So I thought it might be a good idea if I could tell 'em a bit about you.

Charles Such as?

Arthur Well, now—you're a Londoner, aren't you?

Charles I was born in London, yes.

Arthur Then what *are* you? What do you do for a living?

Charles I'm a barrister, but—er—I thought.

Arthur Eh? What?

Charles A barrister, sir.

Arthur (*incredulous*) A barrister?

Charles Of Lincoln's Inn.

Arthur Lincoln's Inn? A barrister? (*His whole attitude changes*) My dear fellow, I'd no idea you were a professional man. No idea at all. Nobody told me that. Good heavens. But how extraordinary!

Charles (*sharply*) In what way, sir?

At this moment, the remainder of the wedding-party passes down the hall from the front door towards the breakfast-room. All sidle past shyly and awkwardly, two men in ill-cut suits of some heavy material wearing white carnations, three women wearing sprays of flowers pinned to their voluminous but shapeless gowns

Arthur You're the same young man that Anna met at the fair, aren't you?

Charles I imagine so. We did first meet at the fair.

Arthur That's right, Mansell. It's in the breakfast-room. You know the way. You just carry on without me—I'll be with you in a moment. Yes—well—when I say extraordinary, all I mean is it's extraordinary that Anna should have—er—been fortunate enough to encounter someone in such good standing as you on a fairground. That's all I mean.

Charles It was quite fortuitous, I agree, but for my part, sir, a very *happy* encounter.

Arthur Oh, but of course. And one that has led on to an equally happy conclusion. Well, you've certainly given me plenty to talk about, but don't worry, my dear fellow. I shall keep it short and sweet. And you, I realize, must be well accustomed to getting up on your feet.

Charles Naturally, I shall welcome an opportunity to thank everyone for all their kindness, and in particular, of course, Mrs Harnham.

Arthur Yes—well, it's quite fair to say that if it hadn't been for Mrs Harnham it's most unlikely that you'd be here today.

Charles I don't doubt that at all, sir.

Arthur There's no blame attaching to Anna, of course—none whatsoever. But the aunt must have been a stupid woman.

Charles I don't quite . . . ?

Arthur I blame the aunt entirely.

Charles What for, sir?

Arthur Why, for not seeing that Anna went to school and learnt to read and write. Ah, here we are.

Sarah enters, carrying a silver tray on which are several glasses of champagne

Sarah (*suppressing a giggle*) Mrs Bradford says she's waiting to cut the cake, sir.

Arthur We're just coming. (*To Charles*) A glass of champagne, my dear fellow?

Charles (*who has been thinking hard*) I beg your pardon?

Arthur A glass of champagne?

Charles Oh. (*Taking a glass*) Oh, thank you.

Arthur (*also taking a glass*) But let me tell you you're not the only one with something to celebrate, is he, Sarah?

Sarah Oh, no, sir.

Arthur This has been a memorable week for Harnham's, too. We are now not only the oldest and the best, but also the biggest, the biggest brewery in the whole of the South-West of England. There! What do you think of that?

Charles I'm interested in what you were saying about the aunt, sir.

Edith enters

Edith Oh, do come along, Arthur. Their glasses are all filled. Everybody's waiting. They want to cut the cake.

Arthur (*finishing his glass and taking another*) We're coming, we're coming. Let's get it over, my dear fellow. Come along. Yes, the biggest in the whole of the South-West of England—that's something, isn't it? And, mark my words in five years . . . I repeat . . . five years we will be the biggest in the whole of England.

Taking their glasses with them, Arthur and Charles go off towards the breakfast-room

Sarah *You* haven't had a glass of champagne yet, ma'am.

Edith (*moving to the windows*) No, thank you, Sarah. I don't want anything just at the moment.

Sarah Mr Mansell's brought a great bag of rice in his pocket, ma'am, so I told him, I said, if *one single speck* of that stuff gets into my hall, I'll scratch your eyes out, I said.

Edith (*from the window*) There's that poor man waiting outside with the fly. If you like, Sarah, you may take *him* a glass of champagne.

Sarah Ooh! It won't make him squiffy, ma'am, will it?

Edith I should hardly think so.

Sarah All the same, I expect he'll say he'd rather have a glass of beer any day, although champagne'll make a nice change for him, won't it, ma'am?

As Sarah moves up into the hall with her tray of glasses, there is a burst of laughter from the wedding-party in the breakfast-room. Sarah puts the tray on the hall table, picks up a single glass and goes off with it to the front door.

Letty enters

Letty Arthur's now in full spate, Edith. Do you want to hear him?

Edith All I want is for them to go. The thing's done. It's over. If only they'd go.

Letty (*gently*) They'll be off presently, Edith.

Edith They should never have come back here. They could so easily have gone straight to the station.

Letty It wouldn't have been quite the same, would it?

Edith It was Arthur, of course. He insisted.

Letty I think he was curious to see the young man. And I must confess so was I. He's—he's very handsome, Edith.

Edith Well, I've done my best for Anna. Now, there's no more I *can* do.

Letty And how pretty she looks, too, in the new clothes you had made for her. Of course, I think it's a pity they weren't married in church, but I suppose it's just as well in the circumstances.

There is a burst of clapping from the wedding-party in the breakfast-room

Sarah, carrying her tray, comes down into the room a step or so

Sarah I give him the champagne, ma'am, and he drunk it down. And do you know what he said? He said, "Very nice, but I'd sooner have a glass of beer any day." I knew that's what he'd say, ma'am. Didn't I say he would?

Sarah goes off with her tray, giggling, towards the breakfast-room

Letty Does that girl sound to you as if she's been helping herself rather too freely, Edith?

Edith So far as I'm concerned, she can fall down in a stupor, if she likes. (*Moving towards the hall*) I shall come down to wish Anna good-bye.

Letty Oh, but won't that look rather . . .

Edith You go and join the others, Letty.

Letty Very well, Edith, but . . .

Edith goes off up the stairs

Letty watches her go anxiously. There is a sustained burst of applause from the wedding-party, followed by a buzz of general chatter, laughter, and the clink of glasses. Letty still stands bewildered

Charles suddenly enters

Charles Oh, Miss Harnham . . . ?

Letty Can I help you, Mr Bradford?

Charles I was wondering where Mrs Harnham was. She seems to have quite disappeared.

Letty She's gone up to her room, but she'll be down presently, Mr Bradford. Is there anything I can do?

Charles I think not, thank you. It's just that Anna and I—well—we've a little surprise for her.

Letty Oh?

Anna enters

Anna Yes, Charles? What is it?

Charles Ah, Anna. My dear, I want you to do something for me.

Anna Anything, Charles—anything in the world.

Charles If Miss Harnham will excuse us both for a moment?

Letty Of course. I should be helping with the guests, in any case.

Letty goes out to rejoin the wedding-party

Anna Well? What am I to do?

Charles First, let me show you something. (*From his pocket he produces a jeweller's box which he opens, showing Anna the contents—a pendant of paste and semi-precious stones*) Look—isn't that pretty?

Anna Oh, Charles! It's lovely. But—oh, my dear, you shouldn't—you've already given me so much.

Charles It's not meant for you, Anna, no.

Anna No? Then who is it for?

Charles It's a present for Mrs Harnham. For all her kindness, a present from us both.

Anna For Mrs Harnham? Yes, yes! Oh, I'm so glad you remembered her, Charles. She'll be so pleased. Now I know what you want me to do. You want me to give it to her.

Charles Not that exactly, Anna.

Anna Oh?

Charles What I'd like you to do is write a little note . . .

Anna (*fearfully*) Write a little note?

Charles Yes—to go with it.

Anna But if we're going to give it to her ourselves, there's no need. We can *say* . . .

Charles (*firmly*) I would like you to write a few lines, Anna. It shows a proper concern and it'll please Mrs Harnham, too. Besides, you can do it so charmingly. (*He moves to the desk and sets the chair for her*) Come and sit here, Anna. It'll only take a you moment, and then we shall have to start thinking about our train.

Like a person going to the scaffold, Anna walks to the desk and sits

That's it. There, now—just a few words of thanks for all her past kindnesses. And try to work in one of those little turns of phrase which I used to find so delightful.

Miserably, Anna takes up the pen. There is a burst of laughter from the wedding-party in the breakfast-room. Charles moves to look out of the window. Anna begins to write, but her eyes fill with tears. At length, she lets her head fall on her arms and breaks into loud, uninhibited sobs. Charles moves to her quickly

Why, Anna—my dear—what on earth's the matter?
Anna (*through her sobs*) I can't do it. I can't.
Charles Oh, nonsense! (*Moving to her*) Of course you can.
Anna (*through her sobs*) I can't. I can't.
Charles Here, let me see what you've done.

Charles takes up Anna's abortive note, an action which triggers off a further outburst of sobbing, and looks at it

Anna (*through her sobs*) Oh, Charles! I—I didn't write those letters. Charles. She did. (*She twists herself round in the chair and grasps Charles about the waist, hiding her face against him*) I'm learning, though. I *am* learning, my dear. You'll forgive me, won't you? You'll forgive me for not telling you before?

Pause

Charles (*gently*) You mustn't cry on your wedding-day, Anna. It's unlucky, they say.

Anna rises and puts her arms round his neck

Anna Oh, Charles, I feel so bad about it. Oh, my dear!

Charles gently removes her arms

Charles You have some things to bring down from upstairs, haven't you?
Anna Yes.
Charles Then dry your eyes, my dear, and go and get ready, for we must be off shortly.
Anna I knew. I knew I was right. I knew it wasn't those old letters.

Tearful still, Anna goes off towards the rear of the house

Charles turns back to the desk and picks up the sheet of paper

Edith starts down the stairs

Charles drops the paper on the desk as she comes into the room

Edith Oh. Anna's not with you, Mr Bradford?

Charles She's just gone to gather her belongings together. It's nearly time for us to go.

Edith Yes, I suppose it must be.

Charles Mrs Harnham—I find it hard to thank you for all you've done, not only for Anna, but for me also.

Edith Please don't try, I—I've done little enough.

Charles (*producing the pendant in its box*) Both Anna and I would be most happy if you'd accept this very inadequate . . .

Edith (*taking the box*) Mr Bradford, this is quite unnecessary. (*Opening the box*) Oh, how lovely!

Charles It's not genuine, I'm afraid, but it looks pretty, I think.

Edith It's most beautiful. I shall always treasure it.

Charles Anna began a little note to go with it. (*He picks it up from the desk*) Unhappily, she didn't get very far.

Edith takes one corner of the note, so that they are both holding it. She glances at it, then their eyes remain fixed on each other. Charles then lets go of the note, leaving it in Edith's hand

So . . . (*Pause*) The letters were yours?

Edith Yes.

Charles No part of them was Anna's?

Edith They were written *for* Anna.

Charles But you wrote them without her—alone?

Edith Some of them. Yes—many. But only on her behalf. I was trying to help her.

Charles Then the thoughts and feelings expressed were yours—not Anna's?

Edith I put down what I would have written had I been in her position.

Charles I see—yes. I think I understand. You had such concern for her.

Edith (*clutching at a straw*) Yes, I had. I *was* concerned for her.

Charles And—quite naturally—you'd no concern for me.

Edith Oh, but I had!

Charles (*shaking his head*) No concern. So—you deceived me.

Edith But it wasn't—I didn't mean . . .

Charles (*interrupting firmly*) You deceived me, Mrs Harnham.

Edith (*almost a whisper*) Yes.

Charles Cleverly. Successfully.

Edith Cleverly? Oh no, no. It wasn't clever, it wasn't that.

Charles To have chained me to a little—peasant——

Edith No! (*She groans*)

Charles —a pretty, little peasant.

Edith Don't!

Charles That was very clever, Mrs Harnham.

Edith It wasn't. It was wrong of me. I'd no intention of hurting you—not *you* . . .

Charles Then why did you do it? (*Pause*) Why?

Edith I began—I think I began in simple kindness. Kindness to her—to Anna. What else could I have done, and then when I knew the girl was in trouble? But I admit I—I went on—for other reasons.

Charles Other reasons?

Edith Yes.

Charles What other reasons?

Edith Writing freely to someone—brought me a sort of—happiness, I think.

Charles Why?

Edith Because—no. No, I mustn't say.

Charles But you must say, Mrs Harnham. Why?

Edith Because—to open my heart to someone—and to find a response— was something I'd never known.

Charles (*after a pause*) Do you mean your letters to me were not all make-believe, that you were not just pretending? Is that what you're saying?

Edith Yes.

Charles You were expressing your true feelings—your true feelings towards me?

Edith Yes.

Charles You meant every word you wrote?

Edith Every word.

Charles And you still do?

Edith With all my heart.

Charles I see. (*Pause*) Well, then—it would appear that you and I are lovers, Mrs Harnham. Lovers by correspondence. In fact, more than lovers now.

Edith Now?

Charles Legally, I've married Anna—God help us both—but in soul and spirit I've married the writer of those letters and no other woman in the world.

Edith But I couldn't—you must know that we could never—ever . . .

Charles (*interrupting*) Why try to dodge the whole truth? You've admitted half of it. I've married you. So let me now make one claim. For the first time—and the last.

Charles moves to within arm's length of Edith and puts out his hand slowly towards her face. Edith is terrified. He suddenly pulls her towards him and kisses her, fiercely. As he does so, there is a burst of loud laughter from the breakfast-room. Edith breaks away from the embrace, bewildered by its ferocity and uncertain of Charles's real feelings

Edith Then—you forgive me?

Charles Forgive you, Mrs Harnham?

Edith Can you?

Charles No. I can never forgive you.

Edith But—perhaps—in time—with Anna, you may find . . .

Charles Never. And with Anna there to remind me, it's unlikely I shall ever forget.

Anna appears in the hallway. She carries her belongings in a small, basket-like trunk held together by a leather strap

Ah—here's my little Mrs Bradford. Are you ready, my dear?
Anna Yes, Charles.
Charles Then we must make a start.

Edith remains silent. Charles takes Anna's luggage from her. Anna runs to Edith and flings her arms about her. The two women hold each other tightly for a moment

Anna exits

Good-bye, Mrs Harnham.

Charles follows Anna off, joining her in the hall

Sarah (*off*) They're going! They're going—everybody! Mr and Mrs Bradford are just going. Come and see them off! Come on, everybody! They're leaving for the station now!

The wedding-party, their former inhibitions now softened by alcohol, troop through the hall laughing and chattering

Edith remains motionless as, to cries of "Good Luck!" and "Every happiness!" and much shouting and laughing, the newly married pair prepare to set forth. Suddenly, as the fly is heard to pull away to a ragged cheer, the new steam roundabout emits three short blasts on its whistle and the organ bursts into gay, martial music

As the wedding-party begins to retrace its steps towards the breakfast-room and the drinks, Arthur comes bustling into the room. He proceeds at once to close the upper sashes of the open windows, thus reducing the sound of the music to a reasonable level

Arthur It's high time they put a stop to this. Come next Michaelmas our new by-laws come into force so they'll have to hold it somewhere out in the country. (*He is moving towards the hallway when a thought strikes him and he turns back to Edith*) I dare say the others will be here for quite a while yet, you know. They're expecting to see something of *you*, Edith, so come along and join in the fun.

Arthur goes off towards the breakfast-room

Edith remains as though turned to stone. The music from the steam-organ swells a little. After a moment—

the CURTAIN *falls quickly*

FURNITURE AND PROPERTY LIST

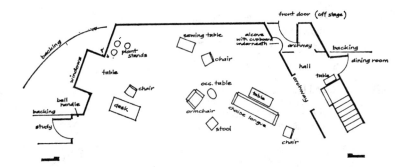

ACT I

Scene 1

On stage: Sheraton desk. *On it:* writing materials, stamps, stamp damper.
In drawers: copy-book, silver coins, smelling-salts, scribbling
block, Charles's letters tied with ribbon—one without envelope
Oval table
Sewing table with sewing materials
Sofa table. *On it:* tray with coffee jug, cream jug, sugar, 2 cups,
2 saucers, 2 spoons
Occasional table
Desk chair
Armchair
3 small chairs
2 plant stands
Cigar stand with cigars and matches
Cupboard. *In it:* Halma game set out. *Above it:* mirror
Hall table. *On it:* rose bowls
On alcove shelf: brandy and sherry decanters, glasses
On shelves various: bric-à-brac, including silver trophies and cups
On walls: oil paintings, including one of Arthur's great-grandfather
On one wall: bell-pull
Carpet
Stair carpet
Heavy window curtains

Off stage: Sheaf of papers (**Arthur**)
Tray with coffee-pot and cup and saucer (**Sarah**)
Goblet of brandy (**Arthur**)

SCENE 2

Strike: Arthur's hat
            Coffee tray and cup
            Brandy glasses
            Documents
            Handbag

Set: Cleaning box and broom in hall
            Brandy decanter with other drinks
            Halma board back in cupboard
            Sewing bag in armchair
            Shopping list on desk

Off stage: Sealed letter (**Sarah**)
            Shopping basket (**Letty**)
            2 lending-library books (**Edith**)
            Opened letter (**Anna**)

SCENE 3

Strike: Letter
            Sewing bag

Set: Sherry decanter back in drinks alcove
            Scribbling block in desk drawer with marked page removed

Off stage: Prayer-book and hymn-book (**Edith**)
            Documents (**Arthur**)

ACT II

SCENE 1

Strike: Bundle of letters—put on prop table
            Handbag and prayer-books

Set: Clean sherry glasses with drinks

Off stage: Bundle of letters (**Edith**)
            Cake-stand with cakes and scones, plates and knives (**Sarah**)
            Tray with teapot, milk, sugar, 2 cups, 2 saucers, 2 spoons (**Sarah**)

Personal: **Charles:** pocket diary

Scene 2

Strike: Cake-stand

Set: Wooden tray with silver cleaning materials on sofa table, place pieces
                 of silver from shelves on it
                 Arthur's hat on hall table
                 Copy-book on desk

Off stage: Documents (**Arthur**)

Scene 3

Set: Copy-book in desk drawer
                 Scribbling pad on desk
                 Flower bowls on sofa table
                 Charles's overnight case in hall

Off stage: Bunch of roses in tissue (**Letty**)
                 Water jug (**Letty**)
                 The Times (**Arthur**)
                 Silver tray with 6 glasses of champagne (**Sarah**)
                 Small wicker trunk (**Anna**)

Personal: **Charles:** pocket-watch, pendant in box, pencil
                 Anna: wedding-ring

LIGHTING PLOT

Practical fittings required: 2 oil lamps (portable)
   Interior. A living-room. The same scene throughout

ACT I, SCENE 1

To open: Effect of cloudless May evening

Cue 1   **Letty** enters with coffee   (Page 9)
           Start slow fade to dusk—brighten fair lights outside window

Cue 2   **Sarah** enters with oil lamp   (Page 10)
           Bring up covering spots in room area

Cue 3   **Sarah** enters with second lamp   (Page 12)
           Bring up covering spots in hall

ACT I, SCENE 2

To open: Effect of morning sunshine

Cue 4   **Edith:** ". . . to post a letter for me, Arthur."   (Page 21)
           Fade to Black-Out

ACT I, SCENE 3

To open: Effect of early evening light

No cues

ACT II, SCENE 1

To open: General effect of mid-afternoon light

No cues

ACT II, SCENE 2

To open: As Act I, Scene 2

Cue 5   **Edith:** "If one knew that . . ."   (Page 50
           Fade to Black-Out

ACT II, SCENE 3

To open: As opening of previous scene

No cues

EFFECTS PLOT

ACT I

SCENE 1

Cue 1   **AS CURTAIN rises**   (Page 1)
Sounds of a fair in full swing, with loud steam-organ music

Cue 2   **Letty closes window**   (Page 2)
Reduce music to quieter level

SCENE 2

No cues

SCENE 3

Cue 3   **Anna:** ". . . she knows all about *them*."   (Page 28)
Gong sounds

ACT II

SCENE 1

Cue 4   **Letty:** ". . . at that would have . . ."   (Page 34)
Bell jangles

SCENE 2

No cues

SCENE 3

Cue 5   **After general exit**   (Page 62)
*Sound of fly moving away, them steam roundabout gives three
short blasts and organ starts up martial music*

Cue 6   **Arthur closes window**   (Page 62)
Reduce music as in Act I, Scene 1

Cue 7   **After Arthur's exit**   (Page 62)
Swell music a little

PRINTED IN GREAT BRITAIN BY
THE LONGDUNN PRESS LTD BRISTOL
MADE IN ENGLAND